THE ESSENTIAL KORAN

ALSO BY THOMAS CLEARY

The Secret of the Golden Flower

The Essential Confucius

The Essential Tao

THE ESSENTIAL KORAN

The Heart of Islam

An Introductory Selection
of Readings from the Qur'an
Translated and Presented

by THOMAS CLEARY

CASTLE BOOKS

KORAN

This edition published by arrangement and with permission of HarperSanFrancisco, a division of Harper Collins, Publishers, Inc. 10 East 53rd Street, New York, NY 10022.

Published by CASTLE BOOKS
A Division of Book Sales, Inc.
114 Northfield Avenue, Edison, New Jersey 08837

ISBN 0-7858-0902-3

Manufactured in the United States of America.

Contents

Introduction

The Qur'an is universally known as the sacred book of Islam, the religion of submission to the will of God. The chapters and verses in this volume of extracts from the Qur'an (the more phonetically accurate designation of the book traditionally known in English as the Koran) have been selected to form a rosary of readings and recitations intended to introduce the non-Muslim reader to the essential wisdom, beauty, and majesty of this sacred book.

The Qur'an is undeniably a book of great importance even to the non-Muslim, perhaps more today than ever, if that is possible. One aspect of Islam that is unexpected and yet appealing to the post-Christian secular mind is the harmonious interplay of faith and reason. Islam does not demand unreasoned belief. Rather, it invites intelligent faith, growing from observation, reflection, and contemplation, beginning with nature and what is all around us. Accordingly, antagonism between religion and science such as that familiar to Westerners is foreign to Islam.

This connection between faith and reason enabled Islamic civilization to absorb and vivify useful knowledge, including that of ancient peoples, whereby it eventually nursed Europe out of the Dark Ages, laying the foundation for the Renaissance. When Europe got on its cultural feet and expelled Islam, however, the European mind was rent by the inability of the Christian church to tolerate the indivisibility of the sacred and the secular that characterized Islam and had enabled Islamic civilization to develop natural science and abstract art as well as philosophy and social science. The result was a painful, ill-fated divorce between science and religion in Europe, one whose consequences have adversely affected the entire world.

In the post-Christian West, where thinking people, including scientists themselves once more, are seeking solutions to the difficulties created by the Christian divorce between religion and science, the Qur'an offers a way to explore an attitude that fully embraces the quest for knowledge and understanding that is the essence of science, while at the same time, and indeed for the same reasons, fully embraces the awe, humility, reverence, and conscience without which "humankind does indeed go too far in considering itself to be self-sufficient" (Qur'an 96:6–7).

Even for the secular Westerner, apart from any question of religious belief or faith, there are immediate benefits to be found in reading the Qur'an. First, in view of the sacredness and vital importance of the Qur'an to approximately one-fifth of all humanity, a thinking citizen of the world can hardly develop a rational and mature social consciousness without considering the message of the Qur'an and its meaning for the Muslim community.

With the fall of communism, it has become particularly clear that global peace, order, and self-determination of peoples cannot be achieved without intelligent respect for Islam and the inalienable right of Muslims to live their religion. The second immediate benefit in reading the Qur'an, therefore, is that it is a necessary step toward the understanding and tolerance without which world peace is in fact inconceivable.

For non-Muslims, one special advantage in reading the Qur'an is that it provides an authentic point of reference from which to examine the biased stereotypes of Islam to which Westerners are habitually exposed. Primary information is essential to distinguish between opinion and fact in a reasonable manner. This exercise may also enable the thinking individual to understand the inherently defective nature of prejudice itself, and thus be the more generally receptive to all information and knowledge of possible use to humankind.

The Qur'an

The name Qur'an means the Recital or the Reading. According to its own word, the Qur'an is a revealed Book in the spiritual tradition of the Torah and Gospel transmitted by Moses and Jesus. Connecting itself and these distinguished predecessors to even earlier dispensations of original religion, the Qur'an represents its teaching as confirming and clarifying the truth of what was in those messages.

The Qur'an is undeniably unique in this tradition, and indeed unique in the entire context of classical sacred tradition throughout the world, in having been revealed in the full light of history, through the offices of a Prophet who was well known.

As the last link in a chain of revelation going back to time immemorial, even to the very origin of humankind, the Qur'an has the special function of recollecting the essential message of all revealed Books and distinguishing this from the opinions and reactions later interpolated into ancient texts whose original dispensation had taken place in remote and even unknown times.

Therefore the Qur'an is not only called the Reading or the Recital but also the Criterion: it is called a Reminder and also a Clarification. A modern descendant of the Prophet Muhammad wrote of this comprehensive scope and function of the Book in these terms:

> The Qur'an is nothing but the old books refined of human alloy, and contains transcendent truths embodied in all sacred scriptures with complete additions, necessary for the development of all human faculties. It repeats truths given in the Holy Vedas, in the Bible, in the words of the Gita, in the sayings of Buddha and all other prophets, and adds what was not in them, and gives new laws to meet the contingencies of the present time when the different members of God's family who lived apart from each other in the days of old revelations had come close one to the other.[1]

Because the Qur'an synthesizes and perfects earlier revelations, its function as a Criterion to distinguish between truth and falsehood is not carried out in the form of dogmatic assertion or condemnation of one religion or another, but in the form of distinction between human artifice and the essential meaning of religion, between hypocrisy and true faith. Thus the same writer explains, "The Qur'an calls itself *Hakam*—'judge,' to decide between Christian and Christian, between Hindu and Hindu, between Buddhist and Buddhist, and so it did."[2] The observation that the Qur'an distinguishes the differences within the adherents of each religious dispensation, rather than among the dispensations themselves per se, seems to be a key to approaching the Qur'an without religious bias.

The Qur'an could not function in this manner in the context of world religions if it were no more than a collection of dogma or the handbook of a particular new sect or cult. The Qur'an speaks to humanity as a whole, to nations, communities, families, and individuals; complete with both an outer teaching and an inner teaching, it speaks both to persons and to souls, individually and collectively. A contemporary descendant of the Prophet writes of the often unsuspected depth, richness, and intrinsic breadth of the Qur'an in these terms:

> For the Sufis of the classical period, the Koran is the encoded document which contains Sufi teachings. Theologians tend to assume that it is capable of interpretation only in a conventionally religious way; historians are inclined to look for earlier literary or religious sources; others for evidence of contemporary events reflected in its pages. For the Sufi, the Koran is a document with numerous levels of transmission, each one of which has a meaning in accordance with the capacity for understanding of the reader. It is this attitude toward the book which made possible the understanding between people who were of nominally Christian, pagan, or Jewish backgrounds—a feeling which the orthodox could not understand. The Koran in one sense is therefore a document of psychological importance.[3]

Here again it can be seen that the very least advantage we can derive from reading the Qur'an is the opportunity to examine our own subjectivity in understanding a text of this nature. This can have important educational consequences, both immediate and long-term, that can hardly be derived simply by imbibing received opinions and attitudes without individual thought and reflection.

The Advent of the Qur'an

As is well known, the Qur'an was revealed through the Prophet Muhammad, who was born around the year 570 C.E. Muhammad was of the noble Quraish clan, the custodians of the sacred shrine of Mecca, believed to have been built by Abraham in the remote past.

Orphaned at an early age, Muhammad developed into a sober and responsible young man, known for his trustworthiness. When he was twenty-five years old, he married his employer, a successful businesswoman most impressed by Muhammad's goodness.

The first revelation came when Muhammad was forty years old, a mature man of impeccable character. It took place during one of his periodic meditation retreats in a mountain cave outside Mecca. Far from inflated by the experience, Muhammad was fearful and demurred; he rushed home to his wife and anxiously revealed what had happened to him. Reminding him of his well-known virtues, she assured him that he was not mad. Then she took him to a cousin, a Christian, who listened to the beginnings of the Recital and declared it to be of the same Truth as that brought by Moses and Jesus.

The first Muslims were members of Muhammad's house. Beside his wife Khaadija, there were the freed slave Zaid and Muhammad's young cousin and future son-in-law Ali. Shortly thereafter Abu Bakr, a longtime friend of Muhammad, also joined the fledgling community of Islam.

After a brief pause, revelations continued, and word of the new Muslim movement soon began to get around. This annoyed the leaders of the Quraish because they felt Islam undermined their authority. Teaching that there can by nature only be one real God, Islam undermined the religious authority of the Quraish as leaders of the old tribal polytheism. Attracting many converts from among slaves and other disenfranchised people, Islam was also seen to undermine the political authority of the dominant clan fathers. Preaching a level of humaneness and social responsibility well above that realized by existing practices, Islam was also seen to diminish the moral stature of the tribal patriarchs.

For ten years Muhammad and the Muslims of Mecca were subjected to abuse and torture. A group of Muslims emigrated to Abyssinia, assured by the Prophet that the king of that land was Christian and would protect them. Eventually the leaders of the Quraish tried to assassinate Muhammad, and so the Prophet was finally forced to flee from Mecca in 622 C.E. This became known as the Year of the Emigration, the year from which all dates in Islamic history are counted.

The persecuted Muslims migrated en masse to Yathrib, later known as Medina al Nabiy, "The City of the Prophet," or simply al Medina, "The City." Hostilities and intrigues against them expanded, however, as the evident moral force of the movement aroused the hopes and fears of increasing numbers of individuals and groups. As a result, during nearly a decade of residence in Medina, Muhammad was repeatedly obliged to lead the Muslims in war. In one battle the Prophet was severely wounded in the head and face, and presumed dead.

At length Muhammad and the Muslims emerged triumphant, not by virtue of a crushing military victory but by constant devotion to Islam and indefatigable resistance to oppression. Poorly armed Muslims would face, and sometimes even defeat, battalions of trained warriors outnumbering them ten to one. And the movement continued to grow, in spite of opposition and hardships.

In the seventh year of the Emigration, Muhammad made the pilgrimage to Mecca, and in the next year the Prophet entered Mecca with a large party of Muslims, unopposed. He cleared the sacred shrine of idols and established worship of the one real God, including the practices of prayer, charity, and fasting. Through the promulgation of the Qur'an and his own example as an inspired Prophet, Muhammad also reformed many aspects of family, social, and economic life.

The Language of the Qur'an

It is generally accepted that the Qur'an cannot be translated in a complete and literal manner because of the intimate relationship between its linguistic form and its semantic content, and because of the incommensurability of Arabic and non-Arabic languages. A modern descendant of the Prophet explains the nature of the sacred language of the Qur'an in these terms:

> Classical Arabic is that version of Arabic which was used by the Koreshite tribe, hereditary guardians of the Temple of Mecca, and to which Mohammed belonged. Long before Arabic became considered a holy tongue because it is the vehicle of the Koran, it was the speech of the sacerdotal class of Mecca, a sanctuary whose religious history legend starts with Adam and Eve. Arabic, most precise and primitive of the Semitic languages, shows signs of being originally a constructed language. It is built up upon mathematical principles—a phenomenon not paralleled by any other language. Sufic analysis of its basic concept groupings shows that especially initiatory or religious, as well as psychological, ideas are collectively associated around a stem in seemingly logical and deliberate fashion which could hardly be fortuitous.[4]

Because this type of concentration, made possible by the nature of the classical Arabic language, cannot be reproduced in English, I have attempted to compensate somewhat by the addition of linguistic notes amplifying the meanings of certain words by reference to their roots and related derivatives. These notes should therefore be viewed as an intrinsic part of the translation itself. The pregnancy of Arabic also makes it possible, and even useful, to render the same word in different ways when translating from Arabic into another language. According to the eminent theologian Al-Ghazali, there is no repetition in the Qur'an, because "repetition" means that no further benefit is conferred; this aspect of language and meaning in the Qur'an also dovetails with the intensive concentration of Arabic that enables a single word to yield a whole group of concepts.

Another distinguished contemporary Muslim scholar and thinker descended from the Prophet describes the language of the Qur'an in terms that seem most directly expressive and experientially oriented, yet also enhance the new reader's sense and appreciation of the unique and inimitable literary qualities of the Qur'an:

> The text of the Qur'an reveals human language crushed by the power of the Divine Word. It is as if human language

> were scattered into a thousand fragments like a wave scattered into drops against the rocks at sea. One feels through the shattering effect left upon the language of the Qur'an, the power of the Divine whence it originated. The Qur'an displays human language with all the weakness inherent in it becoming suddenly the recipient of the Divine Word and displaying its frailty before a power which is infinitely greater than man can imagine.[5]

This "shattered" and "scattered" facade of language is one factor that makes the Qur'an difficult for many Westerners to approach, until the reason for this effect is adequately understood. Then the dramatic shifts in person, mood, tense, and mode become exhilarating exercises in perspective and translation of consciousness into a new manner of perception.

Readings from the Qur'an

For the reasons summarized above, the Qur'an is extremely dense and extraordinarily intense. The present collection of readings from the Qur'an is simply designed to help non-Muslim Westerners approach this sacred book and savor something of its literally amazing power and grace through a selection of chapters and verses encapsulating some of the central ideas and essential beauties of the Book. (Verse numbers appear in parentheses throughout.)

Such is the nature of the Qur'an that many of the variations in literal translations that are as linguistically accurate as can be under the circumstances are present in subtleties, particularly nuances of particles and modal relations. For this reason, most renditions of the Qur'an look much alike to non-Muslim Westerners at first glance. These subtle nuances, however, can be combined in many ways to develop into considerable differences. These differences are intensified, furthermore, in proportion to the measure and degree of concentration and contemplation brought to bear by the individual reader.

Certain characteristics of English also come into play when translating a sacred text into this language. Most significantly, there is the fact that there is no such thing as a sacred English. There is, furthermore, no such thing as a standard English. There is not even a classical English, in the same sense that there is a classical Arabic or a classical Sanskrit. Finally, for the very reason that there is no sacred, standard, or classical English, there is also no universal or even common literary aesthetic in English.

One particular problem in rendering the Qur'an into English is presented by the numerous intensive forms used to refer to attributes of God. There are different forms of intensification in Arabic, with different ways of interpreting or describing even one form. In this English version, general, encompassing terms of intensity are used, with the provision that these expressions are intended to function as points from which the consciousness of the reader is to launch upwards toward contemplation of supernal ideals. The purpose, in other words, is not to represent God in human terms but to use human language as a means of directing the eye of contemplation toward the inexpressible infinity of the spiritual and metaphysical realities symbolized by language.

Another special problem in translating from the Qur'an into modern English is in the treatment of pronominal reference to God. In contemporary English, there is no third person pronoun perfectly well suited to making reference to the transcendent God beyond all human conceptions. The ultimate shortcoming of human language is natural, of course, and not peculiar to English; but there are particular reasons for attending to the problem of the third person pronoun. Many people of Jewish and Christian background feel alienated from their native faiths by what they call the Angry Old Man image of God, with which they have been taught to associate religion. Furthermore, what has been perceived as the masculine bias of this image is particularly well known to have alienated many Western women from monotheism. This would seem to be an unnecessary waste.

To avoid short-circuiting the attention of significant segments of the modern audience at such a rudimentary stage, I have translated the third person Arabic pronoun *huwa/hu* as referring to God as God, or God as Truth, rather than as referring to the English pronouns "He" or "Him." In technical terms, this means that since the fundamental linguistic resource is the power of reference, one technique for handling difficulties in translation begins with considering language from this point of view.

Inasmuch as languages do differ, it is axiomatic that *manners* of reference can never be completely or perfectly aligned from language to language; and therefore the attempt to do so does not in itself reproduce equivalent *powers* of reference. Thus the first priority of translation, in terms of meaning, is to seek to engage the *power* of reference as efficiently as possible, in whatever manner the target language may afford. In this case, the principle means that a pronoun in one language is not taken to refer to a pronoun in another language, but to the original nominal referent for which the pronoun stands, and by which name/noun it can thus be meaningfully translated. In this case, following the injunction of the Qur'an to call God by "the most beautiful names," I have generally rendered pronominal reference to the divine by "God," a name which is in this context uniquely unambiguous.

It should be observed, furthermore, that reference to God in the Qur'an is commonly made in the first person plural, occasionally singular: God often speaks as "We/Us/Our," sometimes as "I/Me/My." God is also addressed as "You," and reference to God may shift through first, second, and third person within a short span of discourse. Humanity also may be addressed as "you" at one moment and then referred to as "they" the next. In this English version, pronominal references to God are thus necessarily capitalized, to make them completely unambiguous. Once it becomes familiar, this shifting of perspective is one of the most interesting aspects of the consciousness engendered by Qur'an reading.

The selections from the Qur'an contained in this book represent what the eminent theologian Al-Ghazali calls the six aims of the Book.[6] The first aim is knowledge of God, including the essence, attributes, and works of God. The second aim is definition of the Path to God, by which the "rust" is removed from the "mirror" of the soul, so that the light of God may be reflected clearly in the purified soul.

The verses of the Qur'an dealing with the first aim, knowledge of God, are called by Al-Ghazali the jewels of the Qur'an. The verses dealing with the second aim, defining the Path to God, are called the pearls of the Qur'an. In giving these epithets to designated verses, Al-Ghazali emphasizes that these two aims, knowledge of God and the way to God, are most important. My rosary of readings from the Qur'an is centered on the jewels and the pearls, containing approximately one-fifth of all the jewels and one-fifth of all the pearls of the Qur'an.

The luster of the jewels and pearls is further highlighted and reflected by the verses representing the other four aims of the Qur'an as defined by Al-Ghazali. The third aim is definition of human conditions at the time of attaining to God. The condition of spiritual fulfillment, of which the epitome is vision of God, is symbolized by the Garden. The condition of spiritual bankruptcy, of which the epitome is alienation from God, is symbolized by Hell, or the Fire.

The fourth aim is definition of the conditions of people who traveled the path to God, such as the prophets of the past, and the conditions of those who deviated from the path to God, such as the tyrants and oppressors of the past. These verses describe the attitudes and behaviors that have, do, and will lead people to felicity and misery.

The fifth aim is definition of the arguments of those who reject truth, proofs against these arguments, and exposure of the inherent falsehood and self-deceit underlying these arguments. The special beauty of these verses is in their demonstration of the self-veiling operation of hypocrisy and specious logic based on unproven assumptions.

The sixth aim is definition of the fulfillment of what is required at each stage of the Path to God, including the manner of preparation for the journey. These verses demonstrate the connection between life in human society and the life of the spirit, how the self and the world may be made into vehicles for the journey to enlightenment and completion.

In stringing these verses together in a rosary for recitation, for the most part I have followed the Arabic original in division of verses. The division of verses into lines, in contrast, has nothing to do with the Arabic original but with the cadence of the English and the psychological weighting of words, which have tremendous individual force in the Qur'an.

In this connection, it is essential to observe that this English version is intentionally designed for reading aloud, for absorption and reflection, because this is characteristic of the Qur'an itself, from the very beginning of its revelation. Reading or recitation of the Qur'an is not supposed to be fast or glib, but measured and attentive, being in and of itself a spiritual exercise. Where possible, I have tried to borrow from the unusual diction of the original Arabic Qur'an (which, it will be remembered, is unique and inimitable even in Arabic itself) for the effect this has on pace, attention, and psychological impact on the intelligent reader.

Notes

1. Sirdar Ikbal Ali Shah, *Islamic Sufism* (New York: Samuel Weiser, 1971), p. 41.
2. Ibid., p. 43.
3. Idries Shah, *The Sufis* (New York and London: Doubleday, 1964), p. 412.
4. Ibid., p. 441.
5. Seyyid Hussein Nasr, *Ideals and Realities of Islam* (London: Allen & Unwin, 1988), pp. 47–48.
6. Muhammad Abul Quasem, *The Jewels of the Qur'an: Al-Ghazali's Theory* (London: Kegan Paul International, 1984), p. 23 *et passim.*

انه لقران كريم

THE ESSENTIAL

KORAN

The Opening

IN THE NAME OF GOD, THE COMPASSIONATE, THE MERCIFUL

All praise belongs to God,
Lord of all worlds,

the Compassionate, the Merciful,

Ruler of Judgment Day.

It is You that we worship,
and to You we appeal for help.

Show us the straight way,

the way of those You have graced,
not of those on whom is Your wrath,
nor of those who wander astray.

The Cow

IN THE NAME OF GOD, THE COMPASSIONATE, THE MERCIFUL

(2–7)

This book, without doubt,
has guidance in it for the conscientious;

those who believe in the unseen,
and steadily practice prayer,
and give of what We have provided them,

and those who believe
what has been sent down to you
and what was sent down before you,
and are certain of the Hereafter.

They follow guidance from their Lord,
and they are the happy ones.

As for the ungrateful who refuse,
it is the same to them
whether you warn them or not;
they do not believe.

God has sealed their hearts
and their hearing,
and covered their eyes;
for them there is a great torment.

(8–20)

And among humankind
are those who say
they believe in God and the Last Day
but they do not believe.

They try to deceive God
and those who believe,
but they do not deceive anyone
except themselves,
although they do not know it.

There is a sickness in their hearts,
and God has made them sicker;
and theirs is a painful torment,
because they were in fact lying.

And when they are told not to make trouble on earth,
they say they are only doing good.

Is it not that they are in fact
the troublemakers,
without even knowing it?

And when it is said to them,
"Believe as the people believe,"
they say, "Shall we believe
as imbeciles believe?"
No, it is they,
they who are the imbeciles,
though they do not know.

And when they encounter
those who believe,
they say, "We believe."
But when they are alone
with their obsessions,
they say,
"We are in fact with you;
we were only joking."

God will make a joke of them,
amplifying their outrages
as they wander astray.

They are the ones
who have bartered
guidance for error:
thus their trade does not profit
and they are not guided.

What they are like
is one who lit a fire,
and when it illumined
everything around,
God took their light
and left them in darkness,
unseeing.

Deaf, dumb, and blind,
they will not get back.

Or like a raincloud
from the sky,
in it darkness,
thunder,
and lightning.
They put their fingers
in their ears
against the peal
in fear of death:
yet God surrounds the ungrateful.

The lightning nearly
takes away their vision.
Every time it sheds light for them,
they walk in it;
and when it grows dark upon them,
they stand still.
And if God willed,
God could remove
their hearing and their seeing:
for God has power over all things.

(21–22)

O People!
Serve your Lord,
who created you
and those before you,
so that you may be conscientious;

who has made the earth a couch for you,
and the heavens a roof,
and who sends water down from the skies,
and who brings forth from it
fruits for your sustenance.
So do not suppose anything to be like God,
when you know.

(28–29)

How can you deny God,
since you were dead
and God gave you life;
and will then kill you,
and then bring you to life;
then you will be returned to God.

God it is who created for you
all that is on the earth,
then turned to the heights
and fashioned them into seven heavens;
and God is completely aware
of all things.

(30–39)

And when your Lord
said to the angels,
"I am placing a deputy on earth,"
they said,
"Will you put someone
who will cause trouble there
and shed blood?
And while we sing Your praise
and glorify You?"
God said, "I know what you do not know."

And God taught Adam
the names, all of them;
then set them before the angels and said,
"Tell me these names,
if you speak the truth."

They said,
"Glory to You!
No knowledge is ours
but what you have taught us.
For You are most knowing,
most wise."

God said,
"Adam, tell them their names."
And when he had told them their names,
God said,
"Did I not tell you
I know the mysteries
of the heavens and the earth?
And I know what you disclose,
and what you have been concealing."

And when We said to the angels,
"Bow to Adam," they bowed,
except one, Ibliis:
he refused, and showed arrogance;
and he was of the ungrateful.

And We said,
"Adam, live in the garden,
you and your wife;
and eat of it comfortably, as you wish.
But do not go near to this tree,
for you would become abusive tyrants."

But then the Obsessor
made them both
slip and fall from there,
and dislodged them
from the state they had been in.
And We said,
"Let you all descend,
with enmity among you.
And there will be housing and food for you
on earth for a while."

Then Adam received instruction
from his Lord,
and God relented toward him;
for God is most relenting,
most merciful.

We said,
"Let all of you descend from there;
but if guidance does indeed
come to you from Me,
then whoever follows My guidance
will have nothing to fear
and will not sorrow.

"And as for those
who ungratefully repudiate Our signs
and accuse them of falsity,
they are the company of the fire;
they are the ones who stay in it."

(42–46)

And do not obscure truth by falsehood,
or knowingly conceal the truth;

and be constant in prayer,
and give charity,
and worship with the worshipful.

Do you command people to be just
when you forget yourselves
even though you read the Book?
Now won't you understand?

And seek help
with patience and prayer;
though it is indeed hard
except for the humble,

those who consider
that they will meet their Lord,
and that they will return to God.

(48)

And be wary of a day
when no soul can compensate
for another soul at all,
and no intercession is accepted from it,
and no ransom is taken from it,
and they will not be helped.

(62)

Be they Muslims, Jews,
Christians, or Sabians,
those who believe in God and the Last Day
and who do good
have their reward with their Lord.
They have nothing to fear,
and they will not sorrow.

(83)

Worship nothing but God;
be good to your parents and relatives,
and to the orphan and the poor.
Speak nicely to people,
be constant in prayer,
and give charity.

(84–85)

And when We took your promise
that you would not shed the blood of your own,
and would not drive your own from their homes,
you then confirmed it,
as you yourselves bear witness.

But then you yourselves
killed your own people,
and drove a group from among you
out of their homes,
assisting efforts against them
with iniquity and enmity.

(87)

We gave Moses the Book,
and caused messengers to follow after him.
And We gave clear proofs
to Jesus son of Mary,
and We strengthened him
with the holy spirit.
Are you not haughty and arrogant
whenever a messenger comes to you
with what your selves do not desire?
Some you have branded liars,
others you have killed.

(90)

Wretched is that for which
they have sold themselves,
that they should reject what God has sent down
in arrogant jealousy that God
should send it down from divine grace
upon whomever of Its servants
God wills.
So they have brought on themselves
wrath upon wrath;
and for the ungrateful
is a humiliating torment.

(102–103)

Solomon was not an ungrateful misbeliever,
but the obsessive were ungrateful and misbelieved;
they taught humanity magic
and what came down
to the angels at Babylon,
Haaruut and Maaruut.
But these two never taught anyone
without saying,
"We are only a test,
so do not be unfaithful."
But then, however, they learned from the two
what would separate man and wife;
yet they hurt no one thereby
except by leave of God.
And they learned what would harm them,
not what would benefit them.
And they already knew
that those who bought it
had no share in the hereafter.
And wretched was that for which
they sold themselves,
if only they knew.

And if only they
had been faithful and conscientious,
the reward from the presence of God
would have surely been better;
if only they had known!

(115–117)

To God belong the East and the West;
and wherever you turn,
there is the Face of God.
For God is omnipresent, all-knowing.

Yet they say God has begotten a son.
Glory to God!
No, to God belongs all
in the heavens and the earth;
everything is obedient to God.

God is the originator
of the heavens and the earth;
and whenever God decrees anything,
God says to it, "Be!"
and it is.

(136)

Say,
"We believe in God,
and what was revealed to us,
and what was revealed to Abraham and Ishmael,
and Isaac and Joseph and the Tribes,
and what was given to Moses and Jesus,
and what was given to the prophets
from their Lord.
And we do not make any distinction
between individuals among them,
for we submit to God."

(163–164)

And your God is one God:
there is no God but The One,
the Compassionate,
the Merciful.

Behold, in the creation
of the heavens and the earth,
and the alternation of night and day,
and the ships that sail on the sea
to profit the people,
and the water God rains from the skies,
thereby enlivening the earth
after it has died,
and spreading animals of all kinds
thereupon,
and in the shifting of the winds
and the clouds
enslaved between the heavens and the earth:
therein are signs
for a discerning people.

(177)

It is not righteous
that you turn your faces
east and west:
but they are righteous
who believe in God
and the last day,
and the angels and the Book,
and the prophets;
and who donate goods and money
for love of God
to relatives and orphans,
and to the poor and the wayfarer,
and to the needy,
and for freeing slaves;
and who are constant in prayer
and give alms for welfare,
and those who fulfill their promises
when they make them,
and who are patient
in suffering, adversity, and hard times.
They are the truthful ones,
and they are the conscientious.

(254)

Faithful believers,
spend of what We have provided for you,
before there comes a day
on which there is no barter
and no friendship
and no mediation.
And it is the ungrateful
who abuse and oppress.

(255)

God!
There is no God but The One,
the Living, the Self-subsistent:
drowsiness does not overtake God,
nor sleep.
To God belongs
what is in the heavens and the earth:
who could there be
who can intercede with God
except by leave of God?
God knows what is in front of them,
and what is behind them;
but they do not comprehend
anything of God's knowledge
except as God wills.
The throne of God
extends over the heavens and the earth,
and the preservation of them both
is not oppressive to God,
for God is most exalted, most sublime.

(256)

There is to be no compulsion in religion.
True direction is in fact distinct from error:
so whoever disbelieves in idols
and believes in God
has taken hold
of the most reliable handle,
which does not break.
For God is all-hearing and all-knowing.

(262–265)

Those who spend their wealth
in the way of God
and then do not follow what they spend
with reminders of their generosity
or with abusive treatment,
they have their reward
with their Lord.
And there is nothing for them to fear,
and they will not sorrow.

Kind and forgiving words
are better than charity
followed by abuse.
And God,
having no needs,
is most supremely clement.

Believers,
do not nullify your charities
by reminders of your generosity,
or by abusive behavior,
as do those who spend their wealth
to be seen by the people,
without believing in God
and the last day.
And what that is like
is a hard stone with dust on it
on which a heavy rain falls
and leaves it barren:
they cannot do a thing
with what they have earned.
And God does not guide
the people who refuse.

And the example of those
who spend their wealth
seeking to please God
and strengthen their souls
is as that
of a garden on a knoll
on which there falls a heavy rain
and it brings forth double its fruits;
or if no heavy rain falls,
then dew.
And God sees whatever you do.

(285–286)

The messenger believes
in what has been revealed to him
from his Lord,
and so do all the faithful.
Each believes in God and God's angels,
and God's Books and God's Envoys.
We do not make a distinction
among individual prophets of God.
And they say,
"We hear and obey.
We ask your forgiveness, our Lord;
for the journey is to You."

God does not compel a soul
to do what is beyond its capacity:
it gets what it has earned,
and is responsible for what it deserves.
Our Lord,
please do not punish us
if we forget or we err.
And please, our Lord,
do not place on us a burden
like that You put
on those before us.
And please, our Lord,
do not make us carry
that for which
we lack the strength.
And please grant us pardon,
and forgive us.
And have mercy on us.
You are our protector;
so help us against
ungrateful people.

The Family of Imraan

IN THE NAME OF GOD, THE COMPASSIONATE, THE MERCIFUL

(2–7)

God:
there is nothing worth worship but God
the Living, the Self-subsistent.

God sent to you the Book with the truth
confirming the truth of what preceded it.
And God sent the Torah and the Gospel before,
as guidance to humankind;
and God sent the Criterion.

Surely for those who reject
the signs of God
there is a torment most severe;
and God is a mighty avenger.

Nothing is concealed from God,
on earth or in heaven.

God it is who forms you
in the wombs,
as God wills:
there is nothing worth worship but God,
the Almighty, the All-wise.

God it is who sent
the Book to you:
in it are verses definitive,
these the matrix of the Book;
while others are metaphorical.
And those in whose hearts is distortion
follow the metaphorical in it seeking discord,
seeking esoteric interpretation.
But no one knows
its original meaning
but God.
And those deeply rooted in knowledge say,
"We believe in it;
all is from God."
But none will be admonished
except for those of heart.

(18–22)

God attests
that there is in fact
nothing worth worship but God,
and so do the angels
and those with knowledge,
standing on justice.
There is nothing worth worship but God,
epitome of power and wisdom.

Indeed, religion with God
is surrender:
and those to whom the Book was given
did not differ
until after knowledge came to them,
out of conceit and envy among them.
And as for those who reject
the signs of God,
God indeed is quick to take account.

And if they dispute with you,
then say,
"I have surrendered my being to God,
and so have those who follow me."
And say to those
to whom the Book has been given,
and to the unlettered folk,
"Do you surrender to God?"
And if they have surrendered,
they are rightly guided.
But if they turn away,
your only responsibility
is to deliver a message;
and God sees the servants of God.

As for those who reject the signs of God
and kill the prophets,
alienated from truth,
and kill those who call for justice from the people,
inform them of an excruciating pain.

They are those whose works are futile
in this world and the hereafter;
and they have no helpers or protectors.

(29–30)

Say,
"Whether you conceal
what is in your hearts
or reveal it,
God knows.
And God knows
what is in the heavens
and what is in the earth;
and God has power over all things.

"On the day when every soul
will be brought face to face
with the good that it has done
and with the evil it has done,
it will wish there were a great distance
between itself and its evil.
And God makes you cautious of God:
and God is gracious to servants."

(42–43)

And the angels said,
"O Mary! God has chosen you
and purified you,
chosen you over the women
of all nations.

"O Mary! Obey your Lord,
humble yourself,
and bow down in prayer
along with the prayerful."

(45)

Behold, the angels said,
"O Mary, God announces good news to you
by a Word from God
named the Messiah, Jesus son of Mary,
honored in this world
and the hereafter,
and among the Intimates."

(48)

"And God will teach him
the Book and wisdom,
the Torah and the Gospel."

(55)

God said,
"Jesus!
I will take you unto Myself,
and I will elevate you to Me
and purify you
from ingrates who disbelieve.
And I will place those who follow you
above those who disbelieve
to the day of resurrection:
then you will all return to Me,
and I will judge among you
regarding that wherein you differed."

(60)

The truth is from your Lord,
so do not be a doubter.

(62)

Indeed, this is the true story;
for there is no god but God,
and God is surely
supreme in power and wisdom.

(79–80)

It is not for a human being
that God should give one the Book
and wisdom and prophethood,
and then one should say to people,
"Be servants to me
instead of God."
Rather be learned in divine law,
for you have taught the Book,
and you have studied.

And one would not instruct you
to take the angels or prophets as lords;
would one instruct you in misbelief
after you have surrendered to God?

(84)

Say, "We believe in God
and what God revealed to us,
and what God revealed to Abraham and Ishmael
and Isaac and Jacob and the Tribes,
and what was given
to Moses and Jesus and the Prophets
from their Lord.
We do not discriminate between
individuals among them;
we surrender to God."

(102–105)

Faithful believers!
Revere God with due reverence,
and do not die
without conscious submission to God.

And hold fast to the rope of God,
all of you,
and do not split up.
And remember God's kindness to you:
for you were enemies,
and God joined your hearts;
and you became brethren
by the grace of God.
And you were on the brink
of a pit of fire,
and God rescued you from it.
Thus does God make evident
the signs of God for you,
so that you may be guided.

And let there be among you
a people who call to good
and enjoin what is worthy
and forbid what is repugnant;
they are the happy ones.

And do not be like those
who divide and differ
after clarifications have come to them;
for theirs is a terrible torment.

(130)

Faithful believers,
do not take usurious interest,
multiplied and compounded;
and be wary of God,
that you may prosper.

(133–137)

And hasten toward forgiveness
from your Lord,
and toward a garden
broad as the heavens and the earth,
prepared for the conscientious,

those who are generous
in good times and in bad,
and who withhold anger,
and who pardon people.
For God loves those who do good.

And those who remember God
and seek forgiveness for their sins
when they have done a dishonorable deed
or wronged their own souls
—and who forgives sins but God?—
and who do not knowingly persist in what they have done.

Their reward is forgiveness from their Lord,
and gardens beneath which rivers flow,
being there forever:
how gracious the reward for workers!

Ways of life have passed away before you,
so travel over the earth and see
how scorners have ended up.

(160)

If God helps you,
then no one can overcome you;
and if God forsakes you,
who could help you then?
So let believers put their trust in God.

(186)

You will surely be tested
in your possessions and your selves.
And you will surely hear many insults
from those to whom the Book was given before you,
and from those who idolize things.
But if you are patient
and conscientious,
then that is the resolve
which will determine affairs.

(188–189)

Do not suppose of those
who rejoice at what they have brought about
and love to be praised for what they have not done,
do not suppose
that they have escaped torment;
for theirs is a painful chastisement.

For to God belongs the dominion
over the heavens and the earth,
and God has power over everything.

(190–191)

Truly in the creation
of the heavens and the earth,
and the alternation of the night and day
are signs for those of heart:

Those who remember God
while they are standing, sitting, and in repose,
and meditate on the creation
of the heavens and the earth:
"Our Lord,
You have not created this in vain.
Glory to You!
Keep us safe
from the torment of fire."

(195)

And their Lord responded to them,
"I certainly do not overlook
the work of any worker among you,
male or female:
you come from one another.
And as for those who have fled
or been driven from their homes
or been hurt in My cause,
or fought or been killed,
I will erase their sins from them
and introduce them to gardens
beneath which rivers flow
as a reward
from the presence of God.
And in the presence of God
is the finest of rewards."

(199–200)

And there are in fact
among people of the Book
those who believe in God
and what was revealed to you
and what was revealed to them,
those who are humble toward God:
they do not sell the signs of God
for a petty price.
They have their reward with their Lord;
and God is quick to account.

Believers,
be patient and persevere,
and be firm and constant:
and be mindful of God,
so that you may prosper happily.

Women

IN THE NAME OF GOD, THE COMPASSIONATE, THE MERCIFUL

(1–10)

O humanity,
be reverent toward your Lord
who created you from one soul
and created its mate from it,
and from these two
disseminated many men and women.
Be reverent toward God
by whom you ask of each other,
and be reverent toward relationships;
for God is watching over you.

And give orphans their property
without exchanging bad for good
or consuming their wealth
commingled with your own,
for that is a grave misdeed.

And if you fear
you may not be able
to do justice by the orphans,
then marry women who please you,
two, three, or four;
but if you fear
you may not be able
to treat them equitably,
then marry one,
or a ward in your custody:
that would be more fitting,
so you do not go awry.

And give the women
their dowries as gifts;
but if they favor you
with anything from it
of their own accord,
then enjoy it
as wholesome and salutary.

And do not give to incompetents
your property that God has granted you for subsistence,
but provide for them from it, and clothe them,
and speak fair words to them.

And test orphans
until they reach the age of marriage;
and if you perceive in them
integrity and reason,
then turn their property over to them.
And do not consume it in extravagance,
or in a hurry before their majority.
And let one who is rich
take nothing from it,
and let one who is poor
partake of it fairly.
And then when you turn over
their property to them,
have evidence or witness made of it,
though God is sufficient
in taking account.

There is a portion for men
from what is left by their parents and closest kin,
and there is a portion for women
from what is left by their parents and closest kin:
whether there is little or much,
there is a determined portion.

And when relatives, orphans, or paupers
are present at the division,
then give them something of it,
and speak fair words to them.

And be as apprehensive as those
who leave behind them helpless children fear for them;
and be wary of God,
and speak to them fittingly.

For surely those who consume
the property of orphans unjustly
only ingest a fire;
and they will be burning
in a furious blaze.

(26–32)

God wants to clarify for you
and guide you in the ways
of those who were before you,
and to turn toward you;
for God is most knowing, most wise.

God wants to turn toward you,
but the wish of those who follow their lusts
is that you turn away,
turn utterly from God.

God wants to lighten your burden,
for humanity was created weak.

O believers!
Do not consume your wealth
among yourselves in vain.
But may there be trade
out of mutual consent among you.
And do not kill yourselves;
for truly God has been merciful to you.

Anyone who does kill
through enmity and oppression
We will expose to fire;
and that is easy for God.

If you avoid the gravest
of what you are forbidden,
We will blot out your sins
and lead you
into a noble entry.

And do not desire that with which
God has graced some of you more than others:
there is a portion for men
from what they have earned,
and there is a portion for women
from what they have earned.
But ask God
from divine bounty,
for God knows everything.

(36–40)

Serve God,
and do not associate
anything with God.
And be good to your parents
and relatives,
and to orphans and paupers,
and to neighbors close by
and neighbors remote,
and to the companion at your side,
and to the traveler,
and to your wards.
For God does not love
the arrogant, the boastful,

those who are avaricious,
or make others avaricious,
and conceal what God has given them
of divine grace.
And
We have prepared
a humiliating torment
for the ungrateful,

and those who spend their money
to be seen by people
without believing in God
or the last day;
and for those to whom
the Perverter is an intimate,
what a wretched companion!

And what burden would it be on them
if they believed in God and the last day
and spent charitably of what God provided them?
And God has complete knowledge of them.

Verily God does not oppress unjustly,
in the slightest measure:
for if there is any good,
God redoubles it,
giving a great reward
from the divine presence.

(48–50)

God does not pardon
setting up partners to God
but pardons anything else
for anyone, by divine will.
And whoever attributes
partners to God
has invented a serious wrong.

Have you not observed
those who commend themselves?
God, on the contrary,
commends whom God will:
and they will not be treated unjustly
in the slightest degree.

Look how they invent
falsehood about God;
and that is sufficient in itself
to be an obvious wrong.

(51–53)

Have you not observed
those to whom was given
a portion of the Book?
They believe in idols and false deities,
and say to skeptics
they are better guided in a way
than are those who believe.

They are those whom God has cursed.
And for those whom God has cursed
you will not find help.

Have they a part in the Dominion?
Well then, look—
They give people nothing.

(58)

God instructs you
to redeem your pledges
to the people due them;
and when you judge between people,
that you judge with justice.
Excellent indeed is that
which God advises you:
for God hears and sees all.

(85–87)

Whoever intercedes
with intervention for good
partakes thereby of it;
and whoever intercedes
with intervention for ill
shares thereby in it:
and it is God
who makes everything happen.

And when you are greeted
with a salutation,
offer a greeting nicer still,
or at least return it;
for God takes account of everything.

There is nothing worth worship but God:
God will gather you together
for the day of resurrection,
in which there can be no doubt.
And who is truer than God in speech!

(97–100)

To those whose lives the angels take
while they are unjust to their own souls,
the angels say,
"What was your situation?"
They say,
"We were oppressed on earth."
The angels say,
"Was not God's earth broad enough
for you to flee?"
And their shelter is hell,
a miserable refuge.

Excepted are the oppressed
men, women, and children
who can do nothing about it
and are not guided in any way:

for them it may be
that God will forgive them,
for God does pardon,
is very forgiving.

And whoever flees
in the cause of God
will find on the earth
many a spacious refuge;
and whoever leaves his home
as a refugee unto God
and the Messenger
and then is overtaken by death
is due his reward from God;
and God is most forgiving,
most merciful.

(105–108)

We have sent the Book
to you with truth,
that you may judge among people
by what God has shown you;
so do not contend
on behalf of the traitorous.

And seek forgiveness of God,
for God is most forgiving,
most merciful.

And do not argue the case
of those who deceive themselves;
for God does not love
the treacherous and evil.

They may hide from the people,
but they do not hide from God;
for God is with them when they scheme
in words God does not sanction.
And God comprehends
whatever they do.

(114)

There is no good
in most of their private conferences,
except those who enjoin
charity or justice
or reconciliation among people:
and whoever does that,
seeking the pleasure of God,
will be given a great reward.

(124–126)

Anyone, male or female,
who does what is good
and is faithful
will enter the Garden
and will not be oppressed at all.

And who is better in religion
than those who surrender
their being to God
and do good
and follow the way of Abraham,
seeking truth?
For God took Abraham
as a friend.

And to God belongs
what is in the heavens
and what is in the earth;
and God encompasses everything.

(152)

For those who believe
in God and the Envoys of God,
and do not discriminate
among the Envoys,
their reward is imminent;
for God is most forgiving,
most merciful.

(163–166)

We have inspired you,
as We inspired Noah
and the prophets after him;
for We inspired Abraham
and Ishmael and Isaac
and Jacob and the Tribes
and Jesus and Job
and Jonas and Aaron
and Solomon;
and We gave David
the Book of Psalms.

And there were messengers
of whom We told you before,
and messengers of whom
we have not told you.
And God spoke directly to Moses.

There were messengers
who brought glad tidings
and who warned,
so humanity might have no dispute
against God
after the messengers.
And God is most mighty, most wise.

But God witnesses
to having revealed to you
God's revelation
by divine knowledge.
And the angels bear witness,
though God
is enough of a witness.

(171–175)

People of the Book,
do not go to excess
in your religion,
and do not say of God
anything but truth.
The Messiah,
Jesus son of Mary,
was only an Envoy of God
and a Word of God
bestowed on Mary,
and a Spirit from God.
So believe in God
and the envoys of God,
and do not speak of a trinity,
for it would be better for you to stop.
God alone is the One worthy of worship:
glory to God,
exalted beyond having a son.
To God belongs all
in the heavens and the earth;
and God is sufficient
to manage it all.

The Messiah
does not disdain
to be a servant of God,
and neither do the intimate angels.
As for those who disdain
the worship of God
and who aggrandize themselves,
God will gather
all of them up.

But to those who believe
and do good works
God will give their rewards
and even more
from divine grace.
And those who are
disdainful and arrogant
God will chastise
with severe torment;
and they will not find
apart from God
a friend or helper for them.

Humanity,
there has come an evident proof
from your Lord:
for We have sent you
a clear light.

So those who believe in God
and cleave to God
will God admit
into mercy from God,
and grace.
And God will guide them
to the divine
in a straight and upright way.

The Table

IN THE NAME OF GOD, THE COMPASSIONATE, THE MERCIFUL

(44)

It is We
who sent the Torah,
in it guidance and light.
The prophets who surrendered to God
judged by it for the Jews,
and so did the rabbis and priests,
since they were entrusted with
the Book of God
and were witnesses to it.
So do not fear people,
but rather fear Me;
and do not sell My signs
for a petty price.
And those who do not judge
by what God has revealed
are ungrateful scorners.

(46–50)

And We caused to follow after them
Jesus son of Mary,
confirming the truth
of the Torah before him;
and we gave him the Gospel,
in it guidance and light,
also confirming the truth
of the Torah before it,
as guidance and admonition
for the conscientious.

And let the people of the Gospel
judge by what God revealed therein;
and those who do not judge
by that which God has revealed,
they are the rebellious.

And We sent the Book to you
with truth, confirming
the scripture before it
and safeguarding it.
So judge between them
by what God has revealed;
and do not follow their desires
away from the truth
that has come to you.
For every one of you
We have established a norm
and an open way.
And if God willed,
you would have been made
a single people;
but God is testing you
in what you have been given.
So race to virtues;
God is your destination, all:
and God will inform you
about that wherein you differed;

and that you should judge between them
by what God has revealed,
and not follow their desires;
and beware of them
lest they seduce you away
from part of what God revealed to you.
And if they turn away,
know that it is just God's wish
to punish them for some of their crimes.
And in fact much of humanity is rebellious.

So do they seek the judgment of ignorance?
And who is better than God at judgment
for a people who are sure?

(54–60)

Believers,
if any of you
turn back from God's religion,
God will bring forth a people
divinely beloved
who love the Divine:
humble to the believers,
strong against the scorners,
they will strive in the way of God
without fear of the censure of critics.
That is the grace of God,
who bestows it on anyone at will;
and God is all-encompassing,
all-knowing.

Your friends in fact
are only God and God's Envoy,
and those who believe,
those who are constant in prayer
and give charity,
bowing to God.

And if any take for friends
God and the Envoy of God
as well as the believers,
truly it is the followers of God
who are the victorious.

Faithful believers,
do not take for friends
those who make of your religion
mockery and sport,
whether they be of those
to whom the Book
was given before you,
or they be disbelievers.
And be wary of God,
if you are believers.

For when you call to prayer,
they take it for mockery and sport;
that is because they are a people
who do not understand.

Say,
"People of the Book!
Do you disavow us for anything
but that we believe in God
and what was sent down to us
and what was sent down before,
and most of you are vicious?"

Say,
"Shall I inform you
of something worse than that
as a reward with God?
Those whom God has cursed,
and with whom God is angry,
of whom God has made apes and swine
and slaves of seducers.
Theirs is an evil state,
and it leads away
from the right path."

(65)

But if only people of the Book
would believe and be conscientious,
We would certainly erase their evils
and admit them to
the Garden of felicity.

(67–69)

Messenger,
convey what is revealed to you
from your Lord;
for if you do not,
you have not conveyed
the divine message.
And God will protect you
from human beings;
for God does not guide
a people who refuse.

Say,
"People of the Book,
you have nothing to stand on
until you practice
the Torah and the Gospel
and what has been sent to you all
from your Lord."
But in most of them
what has been sent
to you from your Lord
increases excess and ingratitude.
So do not grieve
for an ungrateful people.

Indeed, be they Muslims,
Jews, Sabians, or Christians,
those who believe in God
and the final day
and who do good
have nothing to fear,
and they will not grieve.

(87)

And what hinders us
from believing in God
and what has come to us from the Truth?
For we hope that God
will allow us to be
with a people who are good.

Cattle

IN THE NAME OF GOD, THE COMPASSIONATE, THE MERCIFUL

(1–3)

All praise belongs to God,
who created the heavens and earth,
and made the darkness and light;
yet those who are ungrateful
equate others with their Lord.

God it is who created you from clay,
then decided a term.
And there is an appointed term
in the presence of God.
And yet you doubt.

And God is what is worthy of worship
in the heavens and the earth:
God knows your secret
and your manifestation,
and God knows what you deserve.

(11–14)

Say,
"Travel over the earth and see
what became of those
who rejected truth as false."

Say,
"To whom belongs
what is in the heavens and earth?"
Say,
"To God,
self-committed to mercy.
God will surely gather you all
for the day of judgment
in which there is no doubt;
those who have lost their own souls
are those who do not believe.

"And to God belongs all that dwells
in the night and in the day;
and God is all-hearing, all-knowing."

Say,
"Shall I take for friend and protector
any other than God,
creator of the heavens and the earth?
For God feeds but is not fed."
Say,
"I am commanded to be the first
of those who submit to God;
and you should not be idolatrous."

(32)

And the life of this world
is nothing but play and sport:
and indeed the abode hereafter
is best for the conscientious;
so won't you understand?

(38)

And there is no beast upon the earth
nor bird that flies on wings
but forms communities like you:
We have not omitted
anything from the Book;
and after a time
they will be gathered,
called unto their Lord.

(42–48)

And We did send envoys
to communities before you,
and seized them
with misfortune and affliction,
that they might humble themselves.

But why did they not humble themselves
when Our misfortune reached them?
Instead their hearts hardened,
and Obsession made charming to them
what they used to do.

Then when they forgot
what they had been reminded of,
We opened for them
the doors of all things,
till they smiled
at what they had been given.
Unexpectedly We seized them,
and then they despaired.

And so was cut off
the last remnant
of the people who did wrong;
and the praise belongs to God,
Lord of the universe.

Say, "Do you imagine,
should God take your hearing
and your seeing
and seal your hearts,
some god other than God
that will restore them?"
Observe how We explain the Signs,
and yet they turn away.

Say, "Do you think
that if there came to you
the punishment of God,
unexpectedly or obviously,
any will be destroyed except
the people who are unjust?"

We only send the envoys
as bearers of good tidings
and as warners;
so whoever believe
and amend themselves
have nothing to fear
and will not sorrow.

(50–54)

Say, "I do not tell you
I have the treasures of God;
and I do not know the unseen.
And I do not tell you
that I am an angel.
I only follow
what was revealed to me."
Say,
"Are the blind and the seeing equal?
So will you not consider?"

So warn by this those who fear
they'll be gathered to their Lord:
other than God there is for them
no protector and no intercessor;
thus may they be wary.

And do not drive away
those who call upon their Lord
in the morning and the evening
seeking the essence of God:
you are not accountable for them,
and they are not accountable for you.
So if you drive them away,
you will be an oppressor.

And thus have We tried
some of them by others,
that they might say,
"Are these the ones
whom God has graced
from our midst?"
Does not God know best
who are the grateful ones?

And when there come to you
those who believe in Our signs,
say, "Peace upon you."
Your Lord is self-committed to mercy,
so that if any among you
do something bad in ignorance
but then repent and make amends,
assuredly God
is forgiving and merciful.

(56–57)

Say,
"I am forbidden to worship
those upon whom you call
other than God."
Say,
"I do not follow your desires;
I would have strayed in that case,
and would not be among the guided."

Say,
"I act on evidence
from my Lord,
though you consider it false.
I do not have
what you seek to hasten;
God alone has the wisdom.
God tells the truth
and is the best of judges."

(59–60)

For with God
are the keys of the unseen;
no one knows them
but God.
And God knows
what is on the land
and in the sea;
and not a single leaf falls
but God knows it.
And there is not a single grain
in the darknesses of earth,
nor anything green, or withered,
but is in an open Book.

And it is God
who takes your souls by night,
and knows what you have acquired by day;
then resurrects you in it,
that an appointed term
may be fulfilled.
Thence your destination
is to God,
who will then acquaint you
with what you have done.

(95–98)

Surely it is God
who splits the seed and the stone,
bringing the living
from the dead;
and it is God who brings the dead.
from the living.
That is God;
so how can you be deceived?

God causes the dawn to break,
and has made the night for rest,
and the sun and moon for reckoning;
that is the ordering
of the Mighty, the Knowing.

It is God who has made the stars for you
that you may be guided by them
in the darknesses of land and of sea.
We have defined the signs
for a people who discern.

It is God who has produced you all
from a single self;
so here is an abode, and a lodging.
We have defined the signs
for a people who understand.

(114–117)

So shall I seek a judge
other than God,
the very one
who sent the Book to you
clearly explained?
And those to whom
We gave the Book
know it is a revelation
from your Lord
in truth:
so do not be any part
of those who doubt.

And the word of your Lord is fulfilled
in truthfulness and justice:
there is no changing the divine word,
for God is all-hearing, all-knowing.

But if you were to obey
most of those on earth,
they would divert you
from the way of God:
for they follow but conjecture,
and they only tell untruth.

Surely your Lord knows best
who has strayed from the way of God;
and God knows best
who are guided.

(120)

So forsake all sin,
both open and secret;
for those who are guilty of sin
will be recompensed
for what they have gained.

(122)

And can those who were dead
but We brought to life
and gave a light wherewith
to walk among humanity
be as those
who are in the dark
and cannot emerge from it?
Thus for the ungrateful
what they have done
is made to seem pleasing to them.

(130)

Assembly of spirits and humanity!
Did there not come to you
messengers from among you
relating My signs
and warning you
of the meeting
of this day of yours?
They will say,
"We bear witness against ourselves."
For the life of the world
deceived them with vain hopes;
so they testified against themselves
that they had been ungrateful.

(159–160)

As for those who split their religion
and divide up into sects,
you have no part in them at all:
their affair is up to God alone,
who will acquaint them
with what they have been doing.

For those who do good
is ten times that much;
and those who do evil
will not be rewarded
but by its like:
and they will not be wronged.

(162–164)

Say,
"Truly my prayer and total devotion
and my life and my death
are for God,
Lord of the worlds.

"No partner has God:
this am I instructed;
and I am the first of those who submit."

Say,
"Shall I seek a lord
other than God,
who is Lord of all things?
And no soul earns
but what is due it,
and none bears the burden of another.
Ultimately your destination
is to your Lord,
who will acquaint you with
that on which you differed."

The Heights

IN THE NAME OF GOD, THE COMPASSIONATE, THE MERCIFUL

(2–10)

A Book has been sent down to you,
so let there be no constriction
in your chest from it,
that you may warn by it,
a reminder to believers.

Follow what has been sent down
to you all from your Lord,
and follow no protector but God.
Little do you heed.

How many communities have We destroyed
and visited with Our vengeance
in their homes by night
or as they slept by day?

And never was their cry,
when Our vengeance came to them,
anything but "We were wrong!"

And We will question those
to whom the message was sent,
and We will question the messengers.

And we will tell them all with knowledge,
for We are never absent.

And the balance on that day
will be the Truth:
and those whose scales are heavy
are the happy ones.

And those whose scales are light
are those who have lost their own souls
because they mistreated Our signs.

We have established you on earth,
and *We* have provided you livelihood there:
little is your gratitude.

(11–25)

And We created you and formed you:
and then We said to the angels,
"Bow to Adam."
And they bowed, save Ibliis,
who was not of those who bowed.

God said,
"What prevented you from bowing
when I commanded you?"
Ibliis said,
"I am better than he:
You created me of fire,
but You created him of clay."

God said,
"Then descend from here:
it is not for you to exalt yourself here.
Get out then;
for you are among the vile."

Ibliis said,
"Grant me respite
until the day they are resurrected."

God said,
"You shall be of those granted respite."

Ibliis said,
"Then in view of the fact
that You have made me stray,
I will lie in wait for them
on Your righteous path.

"And I intend to come upon them,
to their faces and behind their backs
and from their right and their left:
and You will not find
most of them grateful to You."

God said,
"Get out of here,
despised and rejected:
indeed, if any of them follow you,
I will fill hell with you all.

"But you, Adam,
dwell in the garden,
you and your wife,
and eat of whatever you want;
but do not come near this tree,
lest you become abusive oppressors."

Then the Obsessor
whispered to them suggestions
to expose to them their shame,
which had been hidden from them,
and said,
"Your Lord has only forbidden you this tree
lest you become angels or immortals."

And he swore to them,
"I am a sincere adviser to you."

So he made the two fall
by means of vain hope:
and when they tasted of the tree,
their shame was exposed to them;
and they began to sew together
leaves from the garden
to cover themselves.
And their Lord called to them,
"Did I not forbid you that tree,
and tell you the Obsessor
is clearly inimical to you?"

They said,
"Our Lord!
We have oppressed ourselves!
And if You do not forgive us
and have mercy on us,
We will surely be lost."

God said,
"Descend,
enemies of one another:
there is for you a dwelling on earth
and provisions for a while."

God said,
"There you will live,
and there you will die;
but you will be taken out of there."

(26–31)

Descendants of Adam!
We have sent you clothing
to hide your shame and adorn you;
though the garment of conscience is best.
That is among the signs of God,
so they may take heed.

Descendants of Adam!
Let the Obsessor not tempt you
as when he had your ancestors
expelled from the garden,
stripping from them their clothing
to show them their shame.
Indeed, he sees you,
he and his cohorts,
from where you do not see them:
for We have made obsessions
friends of those without faith.

And when they do what is shameful,
they say, "We found our fathers at it,
and God has directed us to it."
Say, "God does not command
anything that is shameful:
will you say of God
what you do not know?"

Say,
"My Lord has commanded justice,
and to direct your being right to God
in every place of worship;
and call upon God,
true to God in faith:
you shall revert
to how God first made you."

Some God has guided,
while some have deservingly strayed,
for they took to obsessions,
these instead of God,
and think they are the guided ones.

Descendants of Adam,
wear your adornments
at every place of worship,
and eat and drink:
but do not be extravagant,
for God does not love
those who waste.

(33)

Say,
"My Lord has only forbidden
what is shameful, open or secret;
and iniquity, and unjust oppression;
and that you associate anything with God
for which no authority has been revealed;
and that you say of God
what you do not know."

(35–36)

Descendants of Adam!
Whenever a messenger from among you
comes to you relating My signs,
those who are conscientious
and amend their lives
have nothing to fear
and they will not grieve.

But those who repudiate Our signs
and treat them with contempt
are the inhabitants of the fire,
those who remain therein.

(87)

And if there is among you
a group who believes
in what I have been sent with,
and a group who does not believe,
then be patient until God judges between us,
for God is the best of judges.

(94–96)

We never sent a prophet to a city
without afflicting its people
with misery and distress
so that they might become humble.

Then We exchanged advantage for adversity
until they grew, and said,
"Our fathers too were touched by distress and prosperity."
Then We suddenly seized them,
while they were unawares.

But if only the people of the cities
were faithful and conscientious,
We would surely have opened for them
blessings from heaven and earth:
but they repudiated truth as lies,
so We took them to task
for what they did deserve.

(152–153)

As for those who have made idols for themselves,
wrath from their Lord will overtake them,
and degradation in the life of this world:
thus do We pay inventors of lies.

But to those who have done wrong
yet repent thereafter and believe,
your Lord is most forgiving after that,
most merciful.

(155–157)

Moses chose seventy of his people
for an appointment with God:
and when violent shaking seized them,
he said, "My Lord!
If You wished, You could have already
destroyed them, and me as well:
will You destroy us for the deeds
of the ignorant fools among us?
Surely this is but a trial from You,
by which You mislead whomever You will;
and You guide whomever you will.
You are our protector:
so forgive us and have mercy on us;
for You are the best of forgivers.

"And ordain good for us
in this world and the hereafter:
for we have turned to You."
God said,
"I strike with My punishment
whomever I will.
But My mercy extends to all things;
so I will make it the destiny of those
who are conscientious and charitable,
and those who believe in Our signs:

"those who follow the Messenger,
the Unlettered Prophet,
of whom they find notice
in their own writings,
in the Torah and the Gospel:
he directs them to what is fair,
and restrains them from iniquity;
and he makes good things lawful to them,
and prohibits what is bad.
And he relieves them of their burden,
and the yokes that were upon them.
So those who have faith in him,
and who honor and assist him,
and who follow the light
sent down with him—
those are the happy, successful ones."

(172)

When your Lord brought forth
from the offspring of Adam
descendants from their loins
and had them testify
regarding themselves
—"AM I NOT YOUR LORD?"—
They said, "Oh yes! We so testify!"
Lest you say on Judgment Day,
"We were heedless of this!"

(177–181)

A bad example are the people
who have repudiated Our signs,
thus oppressing their own souls.

Those whom God does guide
are thus those rightly guided;
and those God leads astray
are the ones who lose.

And We have made for hell
many sprites and humans:
they have hearts,
but do not understand with them;
and they have eyes,
but do not see with them;
and they have ears,
but do not hear with them.
They are like cattle,
but even more astray;
they are the heedless ones.

The most beautiful names are God's,
so call on God by them,
avoiding those who profane the names:
they will be given their due
for what they have been doing.

And of those We have created
is a people who guide by truth
and with it render justice.

(204–206)

And when the Recital is read,
listen to it silently
that you may be blessed with mercy.

And remember your Lord
within your soul
in humility and awe,
morning and evening,
without ostentation in words;
and do not be of the heedless.

Those with your Lord
are not too arrogant to worship;
they honor and bow to God.

T̲aa Haa

IN THE NAME OF GOD, THE COMPASSIONATE, THE MERCIFUL

(2–8)

We have not sent
the Recital down to you
that you should be miserable,

but only as a reminder
to those who fear God,

a revelation from the Creator
of the earth and the heavens on high,

the Compassionate One
established on the Throne,

to whom belongs whatever
is in the heavens and on earth,
and what is between them,
and what is under the soil.

So if you speak the word aloud,
surely God knows the secret,
and what is most deeply concealed.

God is the only God,
to whom belong the most beautiful names.

(25–36)

[Moses] said, "My Lord,
expand my chest for me,

and ease my task for me,

and loosen the knot from my tongue,

that they may understand my speech.

And provide me a minister
from my family,

Aaron, my brother;

increase my strength by him,

and have him share my task,

that we may glorify You much

and remember You often.

For You are watching over us."

God said, "Moses,
your request is granted."

The Prophets

IN THE NAME OF GOD, THE COMPASSIONATE, THE MERCIFUL

(1–10)

Their reckoning has drawn near for humankind,
while they turn away in heedlessness.

Whenever there comes to them
a new reminder from their Lord,
they ridicule it as they hear it,

their hearts inattentive.
And they keep their conferences secret,
do those who act oppressively:
"Is this but a man like yourselves?
Will you then take to sorcery,
with open eyes?"

[The Prophet] said,
"My Lord knows what is said
in heaven and on earth;
God is all-hearing and all-knowing."

"No," they say, "it is a jumble of dreams."
"No, he made it up."
"No, he is a poet."
"Let him produce a sign
like what was revealed
by the ancients."

No community before them
that We destroyed believed:
will they then believe?

And We never sent before you
any but men whom We inspired:
so ask the people who have been reminded
if you do not know.

And We did not give them bodies
that did not eat food;
and they were not immortal.

Then We fulfilled the promise
and We saved them,
and those We willed to save.
And We destroyed the wasteful,
who went beyond all bounds.

We have sent to you a Book
in which is a reminder for you all:
will you not then comprehend?

(11–29)

How many communities
have We annihilated
as wrongdoers and oppressors,
and produced other peoples after them?

And when they feel Our vengeance,
they flee from it.

Do not flee, but return
to what has been given you
of the good things in this life,
and to your homes,
so that you may be questioned.

They said, "To our dismay,
we were indeed wrongdoers!"

And that did not cease
to be their cry
until We mowed them down,
reduced to dead ashes.

And not in play did We create
heaven and earth
and all that is between them.

Had We wished to take to sport,
We would have made one
from Our Own domain
if We were to do so.

No, but We do hurl
Truth against falsehood,
and It breaks its head,
and falsehood perishes.
And woe to you all
for what you assert.

To God belongs all those
in the heavens and on the earth:
and those in the presence Divine
are not too proud to worship God,
and neither do they weary:

they glorify God unceasingly,
by night and by day.

Have they taken to gods from the earth
who resurrect the dead?

Had there been gods
in heaven and earth
other than The God,
both would surely
have gone to ruin.
So glory to God,
Lord of the Throne,
beyond what they describe.

God is not questioned
for what God does;
they are the ones
to be questioned.

Have they taken to gods
other than The One?
Say, "Bring your proof.
This is the reminder
of those who are with me,
and the reminder
of those before me."
But most of them
do not know the truth,
and so they turn away.

Whenever We sent an envoy,
We revealed to him
that there is nothing to worship
but Me, so worship Me.

Yet they say,
"The Compassionate One has gotten a son;
glory to Him!"
No, they are but honored servants:

they do not speak before God does,
and they act by God's decree.

God knows what lays before them
and what is behind them:
and they do not intercede
but for those with whom God is pleased,
and they are wary for fear of God.

And if any of them say,
"I am to be worshiped instead of God,"
for that We reward them with hell:
thus do we recompense wrongdoers.

(30–41)

Do not the ungrateful perceive
that the heavens and the earth
were united together,
then We split them apart?
And We made from water
all living things.
Will they not have faith?

And We set upon the earth
immovable mountains,
lest it quake with them;
and We set on it pathways as roads,
so that they might be guided.

And We made the sky
a roof, protected;
yet they turn away from its signs.

And God it is who created
the night and the day,
and the sun and the moon,
each swimming in an orbit.

And We have not granted permanence
to anyone before you.
If then you will die,
are they to be here forever?

Every soul experiences death.
And We try you all
by ill and by good
as experiential proof.
And to Us you will all be returned.

And when ingrates without faith see you,
they only take you for a joke:
"Is this the one who mentions your gods?"
While they themselves reject
reminder of The Compassionate One.

Humankind is made of haste.
I will show you all My signs,
so do not try to hurry Me.

And they say,
"When is this promise fulfilled,
if you are being truthful?"

If only disbelievers knew of the time
when they cannot ward off the fire
from their faces or from their backs
and they will not be helped!

No, it will come upon them unawares,
and confound them,
so they cannot avert it,
and no respite will they have.

And Messengers before you
have indeed been mocked;
but the scoffers were surrounded
by what they had been mocking.

(42–50)

Say, "Who can protect you
from the Compassionate One
by night and by day?"
But they turn away
from mention of their Lord.

Have they gods to defend them
instead of Us?
They are unable to help themselves,
and they are not protected from Us.

But We let these people enjoy things,
they and their forefathers,
until life grew long to them.
Do they not then see
that We affect the earth,
reducing it from its borders?
Will they then be the winners?

Say, "I only warn you all by revelation."
But the deaf do not hear the call
when they happen to be warned.

But if there touched them
a breath of the punishment of their Lord,
they would surely say,
"To our dismay, we were doing wrong!"

And We will set up the scales of justice
for the day of reckoning:
and no soul shall be wronged in anything.
And be it the weight of a mustard seed,
We will bring it forth:
and We are well able to take account.

And We gave Moses and Aaron
the Criterion, and Light,
and a reminder for the conscientious,

those who fear their Lord in secret,
and who are dreading the Hour.

And this is a blessed message
We have sent:
will you all then reject it?

Light

IN THE NAME OF GOD, THE COMPASSIONATE, THE MERCIFUL

(35–42)

God is the light
of the heavens and the earth.
The simile of God's light
is like a niche in which is a lamp,
the lamp in a globe of glass,
the globe of glass as if it were a shining star,
lit from a blessed olive tree
neither of the East nor of the West,
its light nearly luminous
even if fire did not touch it.
Light upon light!
God guides to this light
whomever God will:
and God gives people examples;
and God knows all things.

The light is in houses
which God has allowed to be raised
that the name of God be remembered there,
where God is glorified
in the mornings and the evenings,

by people who are not diverted
by business or commerce
from remembrance of God
and persistence in prayer
and giving of alms,
as they fear a day on which
hearts and eyes will be transformed,

that God may reward them
for the best of what they did,
and grant them even more
from the grace divine.
And God provides without measure
to whomever God will.

As for the ungrateful who do not have faith,
their works are like a mirage on a plain,
which the thirsty man thinks to be water
until he comes to it and finds nothing there—
but he finds God in his presence,
and God pays him his earnings;
and God is swift in accounting—

or like the darknesses
in an ocean deep and vast
covered over with waves,
upon them waves,
over them clouds.
Darknesses one on top of another;
if one stretched forth a hand,
one would hardly see it.
And whoever God gives no light
has no light at all.

Do you not see that God is glorified
by all beings in the heavens and the earth,
even the birds on the wing?
Each one knows its own mode
of prayer and of praise:
and God is aware
of all that they do.

For to God belongs the dominion
of the heavens and the earth;
and the journey is to God.

Rome

IN THE NAME OF GOD, THE COMPASSIONATE, THE MERCIFUL

(2–10)

The Roman Empire has been defeated

in the nearest part of earth;
but they will be victors after their defeat,

in three to ten years.
All matters are up to God,
in the past and in the future.
And on that day
the faithful will exult,

with the help of God.
God helps whom God will,
and God is almighty, most merciful.

It is the promise of God:
and God does not break a divine promise,
though most of humanity does not know.

They know the externals
of the life of the world,
but they are heedless
of the ultimate end.

Do they not reflect within their souls?
God did not create the heavens and the earth
and all that is between them
but in the right way and for an appointed term:
but most of humanity does not believe
in the meeting with their Lord.

And do they not travel the earth
and see how those before them ended up?
They were more powerful than these,
and tilled the earth, and populated it,
more densely than have these.
And there came to them
Messengers to them with clarifications.
And God would not wrong them,
but they have wronged themselves.

Then the end of those who did evil was evil,
in that they rejected the signs of God
and took them for a joke.

(11–19)

God initiates creation,
then repeats it;
then to God you are returned.

And on the day the hour arrives,
sinners will be despondent.

And they will have no intercessors
from among their idols,
and they will curse these idols of theirs.

And on the day the hour arrives,
on that day they will be divided:

those who had faith and did good works
will be gladdened in a garden;

while those who disbelieved
and repudiated Our signs and the final meeting
will be brought to punishment.

So glorify God
as you enter into the evenings
and as you enter into the mornings—

for to God belongs all praise
in the heavens and the earth—
and at dusk and noontide.

God brings forth the living from the dead,
and brings forth the dead from the living;
and God enlivens the earth after its death:
and so will you all be brought forth.

(20–27)

And among the signs of God
is creating you all from dust;
and there you are, humankind,
propagating widely.

And among the signs of God
is having created for you
mates from yourselves
that you may feel at home with them,
and God put love and kindness among you.
Surely in that is a sign
for a reflective people.

And among the signs of God
is the creation of the heavens and the earth
and the diversity of your languages and your complexions.
Surely in that is a sign for the knowing.

And among the signs of God
is your sleep by night and by day,
and your seeking from the bounty of God.
Surely in that is a sign for a people who hear.

And among the signs of God
is showing you lightning,
occasion for fear and for hope;
and God sends water
down from the sky,
enlivening the earth
after it has died.
Surely in that is a sign
for an intelligent people.

And among the signs of God
is that sky and earth stand by divine decree.
Then when God calls you
with a call from earth,
you will all come forth.

To God belongs everyone
in the heavens and the earth:
all are obedient to God.

And God it is who begins creation,
then repeats it:
and that is supremely easy for God.
And to God refers the highest ideal
in the heavens and the earth:
and God is almighty, most wise.

(28–40)

God gives you an example
from your own realm:
have you slaves who are partners
in what We have provided for you,
and you are equals in it,
you fearing them as you fear yourselves?
Thus do we explain the signs
to an understanding people.

No, those who do wrong
follow their own desires without knowledge.
Then who guides those whom God has led astray?
There are no helpers for them.

So turn your being to religion
in sincere devotion
by God-given nature,
according to which God created humanity.
There is no changing the nature
created by God.
That is the right religion,
but most of humanity does not know.

Turning to God repentant,
be conscientious and prayerful,
and do not be idolators,

those who splinter their religion
and have become sectarian,
each party delighting in what they have.

And when affliction touches people,
they cry to their Lord, turning repentant to God.
Then when God has made them taste
of mercy from the Divine,
some of them attribute
partners to their Lord,

so that they are ungrateful
for what We have given them.
Enjoy, then, for you will soon know.

Have We sent down to them
an authority who speaks
of what they have idolized?

And when We have people taste mercy,
they rejoice in it;
but if ill befalls them
for what their own hands have brought on,
then they despair.

Do they not see that God
expands and restricts the provision
of whomever God will?
Surely in that is a sign
for a people who believe.

So give their right to kin
and the poor and the wayfarer:
that is best for those who seek
the presence and favor of God;
and they are the ones who thrive.

Whatever you give from excess profit
that it may grow even more
invested in people's wealth
does not increase with God;
but what you give in charity
seeking the presence and favor of God
is what will be compounded.

God is the one who created you all,
then provided you sustenance,
then will cause you to die,
then will bring you to life.
Are there among your idols
any who can do aught of that?
Glory to God, exalted beyond
any association.

(41–60)

Corruption has appeared
on land and on sea
because of what
human hands have earned
to make them taste
some of what they did,
that they may turn back.

Say, "Travel the earth and see
how those before you ended up:
most of them were idolatrous."

So direct your being
to the right religion
before there comes a day from God
that cannot be averted:
on that day they'll be divided.

Those who were ungrateful
bear responsibility for their ingratitude;
while those who do good works
prepare for the repose of their own souls,

that God may requite from the bounty divine
those who have faith and do good works.
Surely God does not love
the ungrateful who disbelieve.

And among the signs of God
is that the winds are sent
as bearers of glad tidings
and to have you taste
of the mercy divine;
and that the ships may sail
by divine decree,
and that you may all seek
from the bounty of God,
and that you may be thankful.

And We have indeed sent before you
Envoys to their people,
who brought them clarifications;
then We took revenge
on those who committed crimes.
And it was incumbent upon us
to help the faithful believers.

God is the one who sends the winds
that stir up a cloud,
and God spreads it in the sky,
according to divine will,
and makes it into pieces,
and you see the rain
issuing from within it.
And it is showered
on whomever God will
from among the servants of God:
then they welcome it,

though earlier on,
before it was sent down upon them,
they were indeed in despair.

So look at the traces of the mercy of God,
how it enlivens the earth after her death.
Indeed, God is the lifegiver to the dead;
and God has power over all things.

And if We sent a wind
and they saw it yellowing,
they would thereafter
surely become ungrateful.

So in fact you cannot cause the dead to hear,
nor can you cause the deaf to hear the call
when they have turned their backs.

And you are not the guide of the blind
out of their error;
you cannot make anyone hear
but those who believe in Our signs
and have submitted.

God is the one who created you all weak,
then gave strength after weakness,
then gave weakness and old age after strength.
God creates whatever God will;
and God is all-knowing, all-powerful.

And on the day the hour arrives
the guilty will swear
they only lingered a while;
that is how deluded they were.

And those to whom was given
knowledge and faith will say,
"In fact you lingered,
according to the Book of God,
until the day of resurrection.
And this is the day of resurrection,
although you have not perceived."

So on that day the excuse of wrongdoers
will not be of use to them,
and no reconciliation is possible for them.

And We have set forth every ideal
for humankind in this Recital:
but if you brought a verse
to ingrates who disbelieve,
they would surely say,
"You are nothing but liars!"

Thus does God stamp the hearts
of those who do not know.

So be patient,
for the promise of God is true.
And let those who are uncertain
not divert you at all.

Luqmaan

IN THE NAME OF GOD, THE COMPASSIONATE, THE MERCIFUL

(2–11)

These are the verses
of the book of Wisdom,

as guidance and mercy
for those who do good:

those who persist in prayer
and give regular charity,
and who are certain of the hereafter.

They are on guidance from their Lord;
and they are the successful ones.

But among humankind are those
who invent amusing tales
to lead astray from the way of God
in the absence of knowledge
and to make light of it.
For them there is a degrading chastisement.

And when Our signs are related to them,
they turn away proudly,
as if they had not heard,
as if there were a burden in their ears:
inform them of an excruciating pain.

Surely for those who have faith
and do good works
there is a garden of felicity,

where they will be forever.
The promise of God is true;
and God is almighty, all-wise.

God created the skies
without supports you can see,
and set upon the earth
immovable mountains
lest it quake with you all;
and dispersed thereupon
every kind of animal.
And We sent water from the sky,
and thus made propagate on earth
every noble pair.

This is the creation of God:
now show me what anyone else has created.
No, those who abuse are in obvious error.

(12–19)

And We gave Luqmaan wisdom
that he would be thankful to God.
And whoever is thankful
is only thankful for his own soul.
And if anyone is ungrateful,
well, God is free from all needs,
worthy of all praise.

And Luqmaan said to his son
by way of admonition to him,
"O my son!
Do not equate anything with God!
For idolatry is a tremendous error!"

And We have made humankind
responsible for their parents—
their mothers carry them,
sapped and weakened,
and their weaning takes two years—
that you should be thankful to Me
and to your parents.
The journey is to Me.

And if the two of them
struggle to have you associate with Me
what you have no knowledge of,
then do not obey them;
but keep company with them in this world,
in a courteous manner.
And follow the path
of those who turn to Me:
then your return is to Me,
and I will inform you
of what you used to do.

"My son! In fact
be there the weight
of a mustard seed,
even in a rock,
or in the skies,
or in the earth,
God will bring it forth:
for God is most subtly aware.

"My son! Practice prayer,
prescribe what is good,
and forbid what is bad.
And patiently tolerate
whatever befalls you:
for that is of the resolve
that determines affairs.

"And do not avert your face from people
in arrogance or contempt,
nor walk haughtily on the earth:
for God loves no conceited braggart.

"Adopt a middle course in your walk,
and lower your voice;
for the worst of sounds
is the braying of an ass."

(20–30)

Have you all not seen
that God made everything
in the heavens and the earth
subservient to you,
and has showered you all
with favor divine
outwardly and inwardly.
But there are people
who dispute about God
while having no knowledge
and no guidance
and no enlightening Book.

And when it is said to them,
"Follow what God has sent down,"
they say, "No!
We will follow what we found
our fathers devoted to."
And even though it is
obsession itself calling them
into the torment of the Blaze?

And those who submit their being to God
and are doers of good
have thus taken hold
of the most trustworthy support.
And the outcome of all things
is ultimately up to God.

And as for those who disbelieve,
do not let their disbelief grieve you.
They will be returned to Us,
and We will inform them
of what they did.
For God is well aware
of the nature of hearts.

We let them enjoy things a little,
then We drive them to a torment severe.

And if you asked them,
"Who created the heavens and the earth?"
they would surely say, "God."
Say, "All praise belongs to God."
But most of them do not know.

To God belongs what is in the heavens and the earth;
surely God is self-sufficient, supremely praiseworthy.

And even if all the trees on earth were pens,
and the ocean ink, backed up by seven more oceans,
the words of God would not be exhausted:
for God is infinite in power and wisdom.

Your creation and resurrection
are but as those of a single soul.
Surely God hears and sees all.

Do you not see that God
causes the night to enter the day
and causes the day to enter the night,
and subordinated the sun and moon,
each coursing till an appointed term,
and God is truly aware of what you do?

That is because God is the Truth,
and whatever else they call on is falsehood;
and God is infinite in loftiness and magnitude.

(31–34)

Do you not see
that the ships sail the ocean
by the grace of God
to show you the signs of God?
Surely in that are signs
for all who are patient and thankful.

And when waves close in over them,
they call on God,
sincere in submitting to God.
And when We deliver them
onto dry land,
then some of them go straight.
And no one denies Our signs
but every traitorous ingrate.

Humanity!
Be wary of your Lord!
And fear a day
when no father can compensate
for his son,
nor a son compensate
for his father,
in anything at all.
Surely the promise of God is true:
so do not let the life of the world delude you,
and do not let delusion
delude you about God.

For indeed it is God
with whom is knowledge of the hour:
and God sends the rain,
and knows what is in all wombs.
And no soul knows
what it will earn tomorrow,
and no soul knows
in what land it will die:
God is all-knowing, completely aware.

Sheba

IN THE NAME OF GOD, THE COMPASSIONATE, THE MERCIFUL

(1–9)

All praise is due to God,
to whom belongs
what is in the heavens
and what is in the earth,
and to whom is due all praise
in the ultimate end.
And God is supremely wise and aware.

God knows what goes into the earth,
and what comes out of it,
and what descends from the sky,
and what ascends to it.
And God is most merciful, most forgiving.

But the ungrateful who disbelieve will say,
"The hour will never come to us."
Say, "Oh, no!
It will surely come to you,
by my Lord,
knower of the unseen,
from whom not an atom is hidden
in all the universe.
And there is nothing smaller than that,
and nothing greater,
but is in a clear Book,

that God may reward
those who have faith and do good:
for them is forgiveness
and a generous provision."

But for those who strive to frustrate Our signs
is chastisement with a painful punishment.

And those who have been given knowledge see
that what has been sent to you from your Lord
is the Truth, and it guides
to the path of God,
supremely powerful,
completely praiseworthy.

And the ungrateful who disbelieve have said,
"Shall we point out to you a man
who will tell you when you are torn apart
and scattered everywhere
that you will be in a new creation?

"Has he invented a lie against God,
or has a spirit possessed him?"
Oh, no!
Those who do not believe
in the hereafter
are in torment
and far astray.

Do they not see
what is before them
and what is after them
of heaven and earth?
If We willed,
We could cause the earth
to swallow them up,
or make a piece of the sky
fall upon them.
Surely in that is a sign
for every servant who turns to God.

(22–30)

Say,
"Call upon those whom you imagine
other than God:
they have not an atom of power
in the heavens or the earth;
and they have no share in either,
and none is a helper of God."

And no intercession can avail with God
except for those permitted:
such that when their hearts
are freed from fear,
they will say,
"What said your Lord?"
They will say,
"The Truth.
And God
is supremely exalted,
supremely great."

Say,
"Who provides you sustenance
from the heavens and the earth?"
Say, "God.
And either you or we
are on guidance
or in evident error."

Say,
"You will not be questioned
about the sins we committed,
and we will not be questioned
about what you do."

Say,
"Our Lord will assemble us,
then judge between us by truth:
and God is the most knowing judge."

Say,
"Show me those you have joined
in partnership with God.
By no means!
No, God is The God,
supreme in power and wisdom."

And We have not sent you
but universally to humankind
bearing glad tidings and warning:
but most of humanity
does not perceive.

And they say,
"When is this promise to be,
if you are truthful?"

Say,
"You have an appointment
on a day you cannot put off
by even an hour
and cannot move forward."

(31–36)

The ungrateful who refuse have said,
"We will not believe
in this Recital, or what preceded it."
If you could only see
when abusers are stood
before their Lord,
throwing back allegations at one another.
Those who had been despised will say to the arrogant,
"If not for you, we would have been believers!"

The arrogant will say to the despised,
"Did we hold you back from the guidance
after it came to you?
No, you were the guilty ones."

And the despised will say to the arrogant,
"No, it was a plot
of the night and the day:
you commanded us to deny God,
and set up idols as equals to God."
And they will show regret
when they see the chastisement:
and We will put yokes
on the necks of the ungrateful;
will they be requited
for anything but what they have done?

And We never sent a warner to a community
but its affluent members say,
"We reject what you were sent with."

And they said,
"We have more wealth and sons,
and we are not to be chastised."

Say,
"My Lord expands or restricts
the sustenance of anyone, at will:
but most of humanity
does not know."

(37–45)

It is not your wealth or your sons
by which you are brought nearer
in proximity to Our Presence:
only people who have faith and do good
are those for whom is compounded reward
for what they have done,
and they'll be secure
in the chambers on high.

And those who strive to thwart Our signs
are brought into the torment.

Say,
"My Lord expands the livelihood
of any servant, at will,
or restricts it:
and whatever you spend,
God replaces it;
and God is the best of providers."

And one day God will gather them together
and then will say to the angels,
"Did these people worship you?"

They will say,
"Glory to You!
You are our Friend,
not they.
But they did worship the spirits,
in whom most of them believed."

Thus on that day
none of you will have any power
over anyone else,
whether helpful or harmful.
And We will say to those who did wrong,
"Taste the torment of the fire,
in which you did not believe."

And when Our clear signs
are recited to them, they say,
"What is this but a man
who wishes to deter you
from what your fathers worshiped?"
And they say,
"What is this but a fabricated lie?"
And those who deny the truth
when it comes to them say,
"This is obvious enchantment."

But We have not given them
Books for them to study,
and We have not sent them
a warner before you.

And their predecessors denied the truth—
and these have not gotten a tenth
of what We gave to those—
and thus they rejected My envoys;
and how was My denial!

(46–54)

Say,
"I only admonish you all on one matter:
that you stand before God,
in pairs or alone,
then reflect:
your companion is not mad,
he is but a warner to you,
in face of severe torment."

Say,
"I do not ask you for recompense:
this is for you all.
My reward is up to God alone;
and God is witness to all things."

Say,
"My Lord hurls the truth,
fully perceiving all secrets."

Say,
"Truth has come.
And falsehood neither creates nor restores."

Say,
"If I have erred,
I just err on my own account;
but if I am guided,
it is by the inspiration
of my Lord to me;
for God is always listening, always near."

If you could only see
when they are smitten with fear
and there is no escape,
and they are seized
from a place nearby!

They will say,
"We certainly believe in God!"
But how could they be receptive
from a state so remote,

having repudiated God before,
hurling insults on the unseen
from a state far away?

There is an obstacle interposed
between them and what they desire,
as was done with their kind before:
indeed, they were in disquieting doubt.

Yaa Siin

IN THE NAME OF GOD, THE COMPASSIONATE, THE MERCIFUL

(1–12)

Yaa Siin

By the Recital, rich in wisdom,

you are surely one of the Messengers,

on a straight path.

It is a revelation sent down
by the Mighty, the Merciful,

so you may warn a people
whose ancestors had not been warned
and so they were heedless.

The word has in fact
proved true against most of them,
but they do not believe.

For We have placed yokes on their necks,
reaching to their chins,
so their heads are forced up:

and We have placed a barrier before them
and a barrier behind them,
and covered them over,
so they do not see.

And it is the same to them
whether you warn them or not:
they do not believe.

You can only warn those
who follow the Reminder
and fear the Compassionate One in secret:
give them news of forgiveness
and a generous, noble reward.

For We give life to the dead,
and We record what they sent before
and what they left after them:
and We have taken account of all things
in a clear book of examples.

(13–32)

Set forth to them a parable,
of the companions of the city
when there came to it
Envoys sent as messengers.

When We first sent them two,
they called them both liars;
so We strengthened the two
with a third.
And they said,
"We are messengers sent to you."

The people said,
"You are nothing but human beings like us.
And the Compassionate One does not send
anything down at all.
You are simply lying."

The messengers said,
"Our Lord knows we are indeed
messengers sent to you.

"And our only obligation
is clear communication."

The people said,
"We see an evil omen in you:
if you do not desist,
we will stone you,
and a painful punishment
will hit you from us."

The messengers said,
"Your evil omen is on your own account;
does it depend on your being admonished?
No, you are a people
exceeding all bounds."

And there came,
from the remotest part of the city,
a man running: he said,
"O my people!
Follow the Messengers:

"Follow those who ask you no reward,
but are themselves guided ones.

"And how could I not serve
the One who created me,
and to whom you will all be returned?

"Shall I take to other gods?
If the Compassionate One wished me ill,
their intercession would avail me nothing,
and they would not deliver me.

"Indeed, I would be in evident error.

"I do believe in your Lord:
so listen to me."

It was said,
"Enter the garden."
He said,
"Ah, would that my people knew

"my Lord has forgiven me
and placed me among the honored ones!"

And We did not send
to his people after him
any hosts from heaven;
and We were not bound to send them.

It was but one single blast:
and they were extinct!

Alas for the servants:
whenever a Messenger comes to them,
they mock him.

Do they not see
how many communities
We destroyed before them?
To them they'll not return.

And each and every one,
all together,
will be brought before Us.

(33–50)

And a sign for them
is the earth when it is dead:
We enliven it
and bring forth grain from it,
of which they partake.

And We have placed on it
gardens of dates and grapes,
and caused springs to flow in it,

that they may eat of its fruits,
though their own hands did not make this:
will they not then be thankful?

Glory to the One
who created mates, all of them,
from what the earth produces,
from their own selves,
and from what they do not know.

And a sign for them is the night,
from which We strip the day,
whereupon they are steeped in darkness.

And the sun courses
in the place established for it:
that is the order decreed
by the Almighty, the All-Knowing.

And for the moon
We have measured phases,
until it returns
to a tiny crescent.

The sun is not to overtake the moon,
nor the night to outstrip the day;
and each swims in an orbit.

And a sign for them
is that We carried their race
in the loaded Ark:

and We made for them
the like of it,
in which they ride.

And if We wished,
We could drown them
so they would have no helper,
and they would not be delivered,

except as a mercy from Us,
and as a temporary provision.

And when it is said to them,
"Be wary of what is before you
and what is behind you,
that you may be favored with mercy,"

not a single one of the signs of their Lord
comes to them without them turning away.

And when it is said to them,
"Spend of what God has provided you,"
those who disbelieve say to those who believe,
"Shall we feed those
whom God could have fed if willing?
You are simply in obvious error."

And they say,
"When is this promise to be fulfilled,
if you are telling the truth?"

They have nothing to look forward to
but a single blast:
it will seize them
even as they are disputing,

so they won't be able
to make their last will,
and they won't return to their families.

(51–67)

And the trumpet will be sounded,
and from the graves to their Lord
they will hasten.

They will say,
"Woe to us!
Who has roused us
from our beds?"
This is what God
The Compassionate has promised,
for the Prophets spoke the truth.

It will be just one single blast,
whereupon all of them
will be brought together before Us.

And on that day
no soul will be wronged in anything,
and you will not be rewarded
except for what you did.

The people of the Garden
will be happy at work that day;

they and their mates
will be in the shade
reclining on couches,

every amenity there for them,
and they have whatever they call for.

Peace:
a word from a merciful Lord.

And stand aside this day,
you who are sinners;

did I not command you,
children of Adam,
not to serve Obsession,
an obvious enemy to you,

and to serve Me,
this being a straight Path?

It has in fact led
a great many of you astray;
did you not understand?

This is hell,
which you were promised:

burn in it today,
for having been ungrateful.

On that day We will seal their mouths,
and their hands will speak to Us,
and their feet will bear witness
to what they have earned.

And if We wished,
We could have put out their eyes;
and they would have rushed for the path,
but how could they see?

And if We wished,
We could have transformed them
in their places,
so they could neither
progress nor go back.

(68–83)

And whomever We grant long life,
We reverse in nature:
so will they not understand?

And We did not teach him poetry,
as it is not proper for him.
This is but a Reminder
and a clear Recital,

to warn those who are alive,
and prove the Word against
the ungrateful who disbelieve.

Have they not seen
that We have created for them,
of what Our hands have made,
cattle, over which they have control?

And We have made them submissive,
so some of them are mounts,
and some of them they eat.

And they have other uses for them,
including milk to drink:
are they not then thankful?

Yet they take to gods
other than The God,
that they might perchance be helped.

They are unable to help them;
but they will be brought forth
as an army against them.

So do not let their speech grieve you,
for We know what they hide
and what they reveal.

Has Man not seen that We
have created him from a drop?
Yet there he is, an open disputer!

And he makes similes for Us,
forgetting his own origin:
he says, "Who can enliven rotten bones?"

Say, "The One who created
them the first time
will bring them to life,
knowing full well
every created nature.

"The One who produced fire
for you from the green tree,
so you yourselves
kindle fire from it.

"Is not the One who created
the heavens and the earth
not able to create their like?"
Oh, yes! For this
is the Supreme Creator,
the Omniscient One.

God's only command,
when willing any thing
is saying to it, "Be!"
—and it is.

So glory to the One
in Whose hand
is the dominion of all things,
and to whom you will all be returned.

Iron

IN THE NAME OF GOD, THE COMPASSIONATE, THE MERCIFUL

(1–10)

Everything in the universe
glorifies God,
for God is almighty, all-wise.

God's is the dominion
of the heavens and the earth:
God gives life, and God kills;
and God has power
over all things.

God is the first and the last,
the manifest and the hidden:
and God has full knowledge
of all things.

God it is who created
the heavens and the earth
in six days,
then sat firm upon the Throne.
God knows what goes into the earth,
and what comes out of it;
what descends from the sky,
and what ascends to it.
And God is with you all
wherever you may be:
and God sees what you do.

To God belongs the dominion
of the heavens and the earth:
and all affairs
are returned to God.

God makes night enter day,
and day enter night;
and God knows
what is in all hearts.

Believe in God
and the Envoy of God,
and spend of that
to which We made you heirs:
for those among you
who believe and who spend
there is a great reward.

What is the matter with you
that you do not believe in God
and the Messenger who calls you
to believe in your Lord?
For God has already taken your agreement
if you are faithful believers.

It is God who sends down
to the servant of the divine
evident signs
to bring you forth
from darkness into light.
And certainly God is in fact
kind and merciful to you.

And what is the matter with you
that you do not spend in the way of God,
though God's is the inheritance
of the heavens and the earth?
Not equal among you
are those who spent and fought
before the victory:
they are greater in rank
than those who spent and fought later on.
But to each God has promised good;
and God is fully aware
of everything you do.

(11–19)

Who is it that will lend
a fair loan to God:
for whom God will redouble it,
and for whom there is a noble reward.

One day you will see
the faithful men and faithful women,
their light streaming before them
and by their right hands:
"Good news for you today:
a Garden
beneath which rivers flow,
abiding forever therein."
That is the Greater Success.

One day the hypocrites, men and women,
will say to the faithful believers,
"Wait for us,
that we may borrow
from your light."
It will be said,
"Turn back behind you
to seek light,"
while a wall will be set up
between them and it,
with a door therein,
within it mercy;
while outside, in front of it,
torment.

They will call to them,
"Were we not with you?"
They will say,
"Yes, indeed, but
you seduced your own selves,
you lay in wait, and you doubted,
and desires deceived you,
until there came the decree of God,
and the Deceiver deceived you
about God.

"So today no ransom
will be accepted from you,
nor from the ungrateful who disbelieve.
Your place is the fire;
that is your master,
and what a miserable destination!"

Has the time not come
for those who believe
that their hearts should be humbled
to remembrance of God
and what God has revealed of Truth;
and that they should not be like those
to whom the Book was given before
but the ages grew so long to them
that their hearts were hardened
and many of them were dissolute.

Know that God enlivens the earth
after it has died:
We have already made clear to you the signs,
that you may understand.

For men who give charity
and women who give charity
and loan a fair loan to God,
it shall be multiplied for them,
and theirs is a noble reward.

And those who believe in God
and the Messengers of God,
they are the truthful
and the witnesses
in the presence of their Lord
They have their reward
and their illumination.
And those who disbelieve
and repudiate Our signs,
they are the inmates of hell fire.

(20–25)

Know that the life of the world
is but diversion and distraction,
ostentation and vying for glory among yourselves,
and striving for more and more wealth and children.
It is like the example of rain,
the growth from which pleases the tillers,
then withers, and you see it yellow:
then it crumbles.
And at the end
is severe torment,
and forgiveness from God,
and acceptance.
And what is the life of the world
but the stuff of deception?

Race to forgiveness
from your Lord,
and to a Garden
wide as sky and earth,
prepared for those who believe
in God and the Envoys of God;
that is the grace of God,
granted to whom God wills.
And God has the Greatest Grace.

No affliction will strike
on earth or in your souls
but is in a Book
before We create it.
Truly that is easy for God,

so that you do not sorrow
over what has passed you by,
and neither exult
over what has come to you.
For God does not love
any arrogant boaster,

those who are avaricious
and urge others to avarice.
And if any turn away,
well, God is the self-sufficient,
the One who deserves all praise.

We have sent Our envoys
with clarifications:
and We sent with them
the Book and the Balance,
that humankind may stand by justice.
And We sent iron,
in which is violent force,
and advantages for humankind,
that God may know
who will be of help
to God and the Envoys of God,
though they are unseen.
Truly God is all-powerful, almighty.

(26–29)

And We sent down Noah and Abraham,
and placed among their descendants
prophecy and the Book,
so some of them were guided;
but many of them were dissolute.

Then We sent Envoys of Ours
to take up after them:
We sent Jesus son of Mary,
giving him the Gospel;
and We put compassion and mercy
in the hearts of those who followed him.
But the monasticism
they invented for themselves
was not prescribed by Us for them:
only seeking the pleasure of God.
And they did not observe it
as it really should be observed.
Yet We gave to those
among them who believed
their recompense;
while many of them are deviants.

Faithful believers,
be wary of God
and believe God's Messenger:
God will give you a double portion
of mercy divine,
and provide you a light
by which to walk;
and God will forgive you.
And God is the epitome
of forgiveness and mercy:

that the people of the Book
may know they have no power
over anything of God's grace;
and that the grace
is in the hand of God,
who gives it to anyone at will.
And God has the Great Grace.

The Spirits

IN THE NAME OF GOD, THE COMPASSIONATE, THE MERCIFUL

(1–19)

Say, "It has been revealed to me
that a group of spirits listened
and said, 'We have heard a wondrous Recital!

'It guides to true direction,
so we surely believe in it;
and we do not equate anyone
with our Lord.

'And exalted is the majesty of our Lord,
who takes neither wife nor son.

'And the fools among us used to declaim
extravagant lies against God;

'but we think no human or spirit
should speak falsely of God.

'Yet there were individual humans
who resorted to individual spirits;
but that increased their folly.

'And they came to suppose,
as did you,
that God would resurrect no one.

'And we pried into the secrets of heaven,
but found it filled
with steadfast guards
and blazing fires.

'And we used to sit
in some of its seats to listen:
but whoever listens now
will find a blaze
lying in wait for him.

'And we do not know if ill is intended
for the inhabitants of earth;
or if their Lord intends right direction for them.

'And some of us are good,
and some of us are otherwise:
we are on divergent paths.

'And we consider ourselves unable
to thwart God on earth;
nor can we thwart God by fleeing.

'And when we heard the Guidance,
we believed in it:
and whoever believes in their Lord
will never be shortchanged
and will not be oppressed.

'And among us are some who surrender to God,
and some who act unjustly.
And those who have surrendered to God,
they seek right direction;

'while those who act unjustly,
they are the firewood of hell.' "

And [say] that if they
had gone straight on the Path,
We would have given them
plenty of water,

that We might try them thereby.
And whoever turn away
from mention of their Lord,
God sends to a torment severe.

And [say] that the houses of worship
are for the only God,
so do not invoke anyone
together with God;

and that when the servant of God
stands to call upon God,
they have nearly become suffocating to him.

(20–28)

Say, "I call only on my Lord,
with whom I associate no one."

Say, "I have no power in me
to do you ill or guide you right."

Say, "No one can deliver me from God,
and I will find no refuge apart from God,

"except reporting from God
and God's messages.
And for whoever disobeys
God and God's envoy,
there is the fire of hell,
wherein they remain forever,"

until, that is, they see
what they were promised:
and they will know
who is weaker in helpers
and who is smaller in numbers.

Say, "I do not know
if what you are promised is near,
or if my Lord has set it a distant time,

"knowing the unseen:
God does not reveal
the unseen mystery divine
to anyone at all,

"except a Messenger
with whom God is pleased;
and God sends forth observers
before and behind him,

"in order to know
if he has delivered
the messages of their Lord.
And God encompasses
all that is with them,
and takes account
of every single thing."

Those Sent Forth

IN THE NAME OF GOD, THE COMPASSIONATE, THE MERCIFUL

(1–40)

By those that are sent forth gently,

then storm tempestuously;

by those who spread an announcement,

then distinguish differentiation

and set forth reminder,

as justification or warning:

what you are promised
will surely take place.

That is when the stars are extinguished

and when the sky is split open,

and when the mountains are pulverized,

and when the Envoys
are appointed their time.

To what day are these deferred?

To the day of judgment.

And what will convey to you
what the day of judgment is?

Woe on that day to those
who rejected truth as false!

Did We not annihilate
peoples of earlier times?

We then cause others to follow them:

thus do We deal with sinners.

Woe on that day to those
who rejected truth as false!

Did We not create you all
from an ignominious fluid,

which We placed
in a secure abode

for a determined measure?

For We have determined measures,
being the best giver of order.

Woe on that day to those
who reject truth as false.

Have We not made the earth
a gathering place

for the living and the dead?

And placed thereupon lofty mountains,
and given you sweet water to drink?

Woe on that day to those
who reject truth as false:

"Go on your way to what
you used to deny as false:

go to a three-forked shadow

that gives no shade
and is no use against the fire

that throws sparks big as buildings,

like a herd of yellow camels."

Woe on that day to those
who reject truth as false:

this is the day
they will be tongue-tied

and not allowed to excuse themselves.

Woe on that day to those
who reject truth as false!

That is the day of judgment,
when We will gather you all
and all of those before you.

So if you have a scheme,
then scheme against Me!

Woe on that day to those
who reject truth as false!

(41–50)

As for the conscientious,
they will be in the midst
of shades and springs,

and fruits such as they want:

"Eat and drink,
as wholesome and beneficial,
for what you have done."

Truly We thus reward
those who are doers of good.

Woe on that day to those
who reject truth as false!

"Eat and enjoy a little:
you are truly sinners."

Woe on that day to those
who reject truth as false!

When it is said to them,
"Bow down,"
they do not prostrate themselves.

Woe on that day to those
who reject truth as false!

In what tale after this
will they then believe?

The Highest

IN THE NAME OF GOD, THE COMPASSIONATE, THE MERCIFUL

(1–19)

Extol the name of your Lord,
the Highest,

who has created
and given proportion,

who has directed
and guided,

who has brought forth pasture

and turned it into brown straw.

We will make you recite
so you will not forget

except what God wills.
For God knows the apparent
and the concealed.

And We ease you
into what is most easy:

so remind,
if reminder avails.

The God-fearing will be reminded,

but the most wretched will turn aside,

those who enter the greatest fire,

where they neither die nor live.

Happy are those
who have purified themselves

and remember the name of their Lord
and pray.

But you prefer the life of the world,

though the Hereafter is better
and more lasting.

This is, in fact,
in the books of the ancients,

the books of Abraham and Moses.

Daybreak

IN THE NAME OF GOD, THE COMPASSIONATE, THE MERCIFUL

(1–5)

By the daybreak,

and Ten Nights,

and the Even and the Odd,

and the night when it passes:

is there in these an oath
to those of understanding?

(14–30)

Your Lord is truly on the watch:

and as for humanity,
when their Lord tests them
by honoring and pampering them,
they say,
"My Lord has honored me!"

And when their Lord tests them
by restricting their livelihood,
then they say,
"My Lord has abased me!"

Oh, no!
But you do not honor orphans

or encourage each other to feed the poor;

and you eat up inheritance
with consuming gluttony,

and you love wealth
with exceeding love.

Oh, no!
When the earth is pulverized,
pounded to dust,

and your Lord comes,
and the angels,
row after row,
rank upon rank,

and on that day
will hell be set forth:
on that day
humankind will remember,
but how will that reminder avail them?

They will say,
"Oh, would that I
had prepared for my life!"

For on that day
no one can inflict
the punishment of God,

and no one can tie
the bonds of God.

O soul,
in satisfied peace,

return to your Lord,
pleased and accepted.

Join the company of My servants,

and enter into My Garden.

The City

IN THE NAME OF GOD, THE COMPASSIONATE, THE MERCIFUL

(1–20)

I swear by this city

—and you are a free dweller in this city—

and by the begetter and the begotten:

surely We have created humanity in difficulty.

Do they think no one has power over them?

They say they have spent much wealth;

do they think no one sees them?

Have we not given them two eyes,

and a tongue, and two lips?

And We showed them
the two highways.

But they have not embarked
upon the steep road.

And what will convey to you
what the steep road is?

Emancipating a slave,

or feeding on a day of hunger

an orphaned relative

or a pauper in misery.

Then one will be of those who believe,
and enjoin patience on one another,
and exhort each other to kindness:

they are the company on the Right Hand.

But those who repudiate our signs,
they are the company on the Left Hand:

over them will be a vault of fire.

Night

IN THE NAME OF GOD, THE COMPASSIONATE, THE MERCIFUL

(1–21)

By the night when it is dark,

and the day when it is light,

and the creation of male and female,

your endeavors are surely diverse.

As for those who give
and are conscientious

and believe in good and right,

We will facilitate ease for them.

As for those who are stingy
and complacently satiated

and repudiate good and right,

We will facilitate hardship for them.

And their wealth does not profit them
when they fall.

For guidance is up to Us,

and the hereafter and this world are Ours.

So I warn you all of a fiercely blazing fire:

none shall enter it but the most villainous,

who repudiate the truth and turn away.

And the most conscientious keep out of it,

they who give of their wealth to become pure,

without having any favor
to be repaid to anyone,

but only desiring the acceptance
of their Lord, the Most High,

who will surely be pleased.

The Forenoon

IN THE NAME OF GOD, THE COMPASSIONATE, THE MERCIFUL

(1–11)

By the forenoon, bright,

and the night
when dark and quiet,

your Lord has not abandoned you
and does not despise you.

Surely hereafter is better for you
than what was before.

And your Lord will surely give to you,
and you will be pleased.

Did God not find you orphaned,
and provide you refuge?

And find you wandering,
and guide you?

And find you needy,
and enrich you?

So do not oppress the orphan,

or refuse the one who seeks.

And tell of the bounty of your Lord.

The Expansion

IN THE NAME OF GOD, THE COMPASSIONATE, THE MERCIFUL

(1–8)

Have We not expanded
your chest for you?

And removed your
back-breaking burden from you?

And raised your repute for you?

For truly relief comes with distress;

indeed, with distress comes relief.

So when you are finished,
be diligent still,

and be attentive
to your Lord.

Recite!

IN THE NAME OF GOD, THE COMPASSIONATE, THE MERCIFUL

(1–19)

Recite,
in the name of your Lord,
who created:

who created humankind
from a clot of blood.

Recite,
for your Lord is most generous,

who taught by the pen,

taught humankind
what it did not know.

Oh, no!
Humankind does indeed go too far

in regarding itself as self-sufficient:

in fact the return is to your Lord.

Do you see the one who forbids

the servant from prayer?

Do you see if he is on guidance,

or directs others to be conscientious?

Do you see if he repudiates truth and turns away?

Does he not know God sees?

Oh, no!
If he does not desist,
We will drag him by the forelock,

a lying, sinning forelock.

Let him call upon his associates then:

We will call the keepers of hell.

Oh, no!
Do not obey him:
bow down and draw closer to God.

The Night of Power

IN THE NAME OF GOD, THE COMPASSIONATE, THE MERCIFUL

(1–5)

Verily We have sent this
in the Night of Power.

And what will convey to you
what the Night of Power is?

The Night of Power is better
than a thousand months:

the angels and the Spirit descend in it,
by permission of their Lord,
for everything that matters.

It is Peace:
this until the rise of daybreak.

The Shock

IN THE NAME OF GOD, THE COMPASSIONATE, THE MERCIFUL

(1–8)

When the earth convulses
in her shock,

and the earth disgorges
her burdens,

and the people say,
"What is wrong with her?"

that day she will tell her news,

that your Lord has inspired her.

On that day humankind
will go forth divided
to be shown their works.

Thus whoever has done
an atom of good
will see it.

And whoever has done
an atom of evil
will see it.

The Charging Mares

IN THE NAME OF GOD, THE COMPASSIONATE, THE MERCIFUL

(1–11)

By the charging mares as they pant,

striking sparks of fire,

mares on a morning charge,

leaving dust behind them,

plunged into the midst of a multitude.

Humanity is indeed
ungrateful to its Lord,

and indeed bears witness to that fact,

and indeed is vehement in love of goods.

Do they not know
when what is in the tombs is scattered

and what is in the hearts called forth,

their Lord surely knows all about them
on that day.

The Calamity

IN THE NAME OF GOD, THE COMPASSIONATE, THE MERCIFUL

(1–11)

The Calamity!

What is the Calamity,

and what will convey to you
what the Calamity is?

A day when humankind
will be like scattered moths,

and the mountains like carded wood.

And as for those
whose balance is heavy,

they will be in a contented life;

and as for those
whose balance is light,

their place will be an abyss.

And what will convey to you
what this is?

A raging fire.

Vying for More and More

IN THE NAME OF GOD, THE COMPASSIONATE, THE MERCIFUL

(1–8)

Vying for more and more
diverts you

until you go to the tombs.

But you will know;

indeed, on the contrary,
you will know.

But if you knew
with certain knowledge,

you would surely see hellfire;

and you would see it
with the eye of certainty.

Then you will be questioned
about comfort on that day.

The Epoch

IN THE NAME OF GOD, THE COMPASSIONATE, THE MERCIFUL

(1–3)

By the epoch,

humanity is indeed at a loss,

except those who have faith
and do good works,
and enjoin truth and justice
upon one other
and enjoin patience
upon one another.

The Slanderer

IN THE NAME OF GOD, THE COMPASSIONATE, THE MERCIFUL

(1–9)

Woe to every slandering caviler

who gathers wealth
and stores it up,

figuring his wealth
will make him last.

No indeed!
He will be hurled
into the Shattering.

And what will convey to you
what the Shattering is?

It is the fire of God alight,

that rises to the hearts.

Verily it forms a cover over them

in towering columns.

The Elephants

IN THE NAME OF GOD, THE COMPASSIONATE, THE MERCIFUL

(1–5)

Have you not seen what your Lord
did to those with the elephants?

Did God not foil their scheme,

sending flocks of birds against them,

bombarding them
with stones of baked clay?

That made them like stripped cornstalks
whose fruits have been consumed.

The Quraish

IN THE NAME OF GOD, THE COMPASSIONATE, THE MERCIFUL

(1–4)

As for the Quraish compact,

their cooperation on journeys
winter and summer,

let them serve the Lord of this house,

who feeds them lest they hunger
and gives them security from fear.

Needs

IN THE NAME OF GOD, THE COMPASSIONATE, THE MERCIFUL

(1–7)

Do you see the one who repudiates religion?

He is the one who rebuffs the orphan

and does not encourage feeding the poor.

So woe to those who pray

without paying attention to their prayers;

those who appear to pray

but are depriving the needy.

Help

IN THE NAME OF GOD, THE COMPASSIONATE, THE MERCIFUL

(1–3)

When the help of God comes,
and victory,

and you have seen the people
enter the religion of God in droves,

praise your Lord
and seek forgiveness of God:
for God is most forgiving.

Flame

IN THE NAME OF GOD, THE COMPASSIONATE, THE MERCIFUL

(1–5)

Moribund are the hands of the inflamed,
and moribund is he.

His wealth does not enrich him
and does not profit him.

He will burn in a flaming fire,

with his wife bringing the firewood,

a rope around her neck.

Pure Truth

IN THE NAME OF GOD, THE COMPASSIONATE, THE MERCIFUL

(1–4)

Say,
"It is God, Unique,

God the Ultimate.

God does not reproduce
and is not reproduced.

And there is nothing at all
equivalent to God."

The Dawn

IN THE NAME OF GOD, THE COMPASSIONATE, THE MERCIFUL

(1–5)

Say,
"I take refuge
in the Lord of the dawn

from the evil
of what it created,

and from the evil
of darkness when it is encompassing,

and from the evil
of cursers,

and from the evil of the envious
when they envy."

Humankind

IN THE NAME OF GOD, THE COMPASSIONATE, THE MERCIFUL

(1–6)

Say,
"I take refuge
in the Lord of humankind,

the Ruler of humankind,

the God of humankind,

from the evil of insidious suggestion

that whispers in human hearts

from demonic and human sources."

Notes

The Opening (al Faatiha) (Chapter 1)

"The Opening" is sometimes compared to the Lord's Prayer of Jesus, in terms of its popularity. The Prophet himself is said to have declared The Opening to be the best of chapters in the Qur'an. Its seven verses are the most often repeated lines of the Qur'an, and it introduces some of the most frequently used epithets of God.

2 "All praise belongs to God" (*al hamdu li l Laah*): The definite article here is understood to make a categorical statement; as the source of all there is, God alone is ultimately worthy of praise. Praise is an aspect of gratitude, which according to Al-Ghazali constitutes half of the "straight way" to God.

"Lord of all worlds" (*Rabbi l !aalamiina*): The word for "Lord" is from the root R-B-B, whose primitive verb means to be master, to be lord, to have possession of, to control, to have command or authority over. The word for "world," which in the definite plural means universe or cosmos, comes from the same root as "knowledge" and "distinguishing mark" (!-L-M), a fact of great interest from the point of view of the Buddhist philosophy of *vijnaptimaatratataa*, or "representation only," which states that the world as we cognize it consists of representations, or mental constructs. The Sufi giant Muhiyuddin Ibn al Arabi also writes in his *Fuhuus al Hikaam* that the created universe is essentially imagination.

3 "The Compassionate, The Merciful" (*ar Rahmaan ar Rahiim*): These names of God are intensive derivatives of the root R-H-M, which suggests compassion and mercy. I have translated the definite article as indicating God to be characterized by the epitome of these qualities, whose intensive forms refer to the exaltation of God infinitely beyond corresponding human qualities or, subjectively, elevation of contemplation to the ideal perfection of God. Compassion and Mercy refer to universal and particularized aspects of divine bounty. Al-Ghazali makes much of the fact that

the Qur'an begins with mention of the compassionate and merciful attribute of God, which qualities he says inherently necessitate all the other attributes of God and are thus mentioned first in the Qur'an. The universal "compassion" of God is the reason everything exists; the particularized "mercy" of God is the providential manifestation of the bounty of the source of being.

6 "Show us the straight way" (*ihdinaa as siraat al mustaqiim*): The word for "straight," *mustaqiim*, comes from the root Q-W-M, which in its primitive form has meanings such as stand erect, perform, accomplish. *Mustaqiim*, present active participle of the eighth measure of this root, has such nuances as upright, straight, correct, sound, in order, even, regular, symmetrical, proportionate, harmonious, honest, straightforward, righteous, honorable: all of these senses should be read into the expression "straight way" as used in the Qur'an.

The Cow (al Baqara) (Chapter 2)

The revelation of "The Cow" began in the first year of the Prophet's emigration to Medina and was completed near the end of his mission.

2 "This book, without doubt, has guidance in it . . .": This may also be read, "This is The Book, without a doubt, in it guidance. . . ."

"conscientious" (*muttaqiina*): This is from the root W-Q-Y, which has primitive meanings of guarding, preserving, safeguarding, protecting. *Muttaqiina* comes from the fifth or eighth measure of the root and means to beware, be wary, be on guard, protect oneself, and fear the wrath of God. I have used the word "conscientious" to render this on many occasions, because its original meaning does combine these ideas fairly well and because the word "conscientious" has weakened to such a degree in contemporary usage that the connection between duty to God and duty to humanity is no longer clear and needs to be revitalized by using the word in such a way as to retrieve its original meaning and force. Elsewhere, according to specific circumstances, I have also used the expressions "reverent toward God" and "wary of God" to render the same measures of the same root, but I do not think these expressions are complete or compelling enough in current idiom to warrant missing the opportunity to restore fuller sense to "conscientious" by appropriate usage in rendering passages from the Qur'an into modern English.

3 "those who believe in the unseen": One of the manifestations of human arrogance is to believe our knowledge coterminous with reality, to assume that there is nothing of meaning or worth beyond our conception or ken. In Muslim tradition it is said that the confession "God knows better" (or "God is more knowing") is itself part of knowledge; realization of the nothingness of human knowledge in respect to divine knowledge is a kind of deep humility that helps the wayfarer overcome the limitations of human self-reflection and rise to reflection on God, and ultimately reflection of God.

"steadfastly practice prayer": The word for "steadfastly practice," *yuqiimu,* also comes from the Q-W-M root noted earlier. Here the verb is derived from the fourth measure of the root, which includes such meanings as straighten, put in order, resurrect, call into being, start, animate, celebrate, persist, occupy oneself constantly with something. Prayer is one of the pillars of Islam, an essential part of inner and outer life, a way of regularly cleaning the mind of worldly preoccupations and revivifying remembrance of greater reality.

"and give of what We have provided them": Islamic thinking gratefully recognizes the privilege of enjoying the good things of this world; the responsibility of sharing blessings is part of the natural pattern of this phenomenon. This is why even good things are spoken of as a trial or a test for humanity. The ancient Chinese classic *I Ching* says, "Those above secure their homes by kindness to those below."

4 "what has been sent down to you": Here "you" refers to Muhammad the Prophet and also in general to those who encounter the Qur'an. Accordingly, "what has been sent down before you" refers to earlier revelations, such as the Torah and the Gospel. It should be noted, however, that the Gospel, meaning the revelation entrusted to Jesus, which the Qur'an refers to as the *Injiil,* is not considered exactly identical to the Christian New Testament as a whole, nor to the Four Gospels as they are now found in the Christian Bible.

"the Hereafter" (*al'Aakhira*): or "The End." This refers to final accounting and recompense. These experiences, including the concomitant experiences of time itself and its cessation, are naturally felt and interpreted in different ways according to different levels of consciousness and understanding.

5 "the happy ones" (*al mufliẖuuna*): This word is derived from the root F-L-H̱, which in its primitive form means to plow, till, cultivate; "happy" comes from the fourth measure, which means to prosper, thrive, be successful, become happy. The idea is that real prosperity is not just material but has a spiritual dimension, which is in fact what gives overall meaning and coherence to the strivings and achievements of life in the world.

6 "the ungrateful who refuse" (*alladhiina kafaruu*): The root K-F-R, here in its first measure, means to deny (God), be ungrateful, be impious, disbelieve. Gratitude, belief, and faith are so important to the Islamic relationship to God and the gifts of God that I have often included both ideas of ingratitude and repudiation in rendering derivatives of K-F-R throughout these readings from the Qur'an.

"it is the same to them whether you warn them or not": Muhammad's mission was "only to deliver a clear message," not to coerce people into professing belief; whether or not someone believes is a matter that is up to God and the God-given reason and free will of the individual.

7 "God has sealed their hearts": The created world acts as a veil to those whose attention is fixated thereupon, blocking them from perception of reality beyond the immediate concerns of this life.

"for them there is a great torment": This is the torment of being blocked from real truth, in which alone are found certainty and peace.

10 "There is a sickness in their hearts, and God has made them sicker": Those who pretend to piety and godliness but are really unregenerate worldlings are not improved by their association with religion. On the contrary, the complacency and pride they derive from their association with religion actually magnifies their flaws. The deceit of false religion carries a "painful torment" because it separates people from truth to begin with, and then its false conceits fail people and let them down in the end.

11–12 "make trouble": This expression is derived from the root F-S-D, which in the first measure means to be or become bad, rotten, spoiled, corrupt, unsound, false, wrong. Here it is derived from the fourth measure, which means to spoil, deprave, corrupt, demoralize, pervert, distort, ruin, foil, undermine, weaken, thwart. Pious fools and hypocrites pretending to be faithful believers may cause all sorts of degradation and corruption by their falsehoods, even without realizing it, being mesmerized by their own facades.

13 "imbeciles" (*sufahaa'*; singular *safiih*): This means fools, foolish, silly, ignorant, stupid, incompetent. Those whose professed belief is a food for their own arrogance think of surrender to the will of God as the religion of simpletons, but their overestimation of themselves makes them the real fools.

14 "obsessions" (*shayaat̲iin*, plural of *shayt̲aan*): From this is derived English Satan, one of the names of the devil. This Arabic name comes from a root meaning to be perverse or obstinate (the essential characteristics of obsession), referring to the satanic rebellion against God, manifest as arrogance, ingratitude, and possessive obsession with things of the world. Another name of the devil comes from the root W-S-W-S, which has the meanings of whispering or suggestion, referring to obsession as the epitome of the satanic characteristic and the activity. This particular verse depicts fools who publicly declare their faith in God, yet privately declare their devotion to their personal idols and obsessions, be it status, wealth, or anything else that may preoccupy the mind.

15 The very levity with which hypocrites and fools treat their religion, as a profession without a reality, lets them go all the further both in the outrages committed openly under the guise of piety and those committed covertly on the prompting of private obsessions. "Outrages" renders *t̲ughyaan*, from the verbal root T̲-GH-Y, meaning transgress, exceed proper bounds, wander from the proper orbit, be excessive, be tyrannical or cruel, oppress, terrorize.

17 This describes the unreliable light of artificial knowledge, of which false religion is one variety. "God took their light" in the sense that falsehood does not stand in the presence of reality; subjective

projections do not remain intact in the face of objective truth; finite man-made thought fails to apprehend the infinite in itself.

18 "They will not get back" to reality, or their source, as long as they are totally preoccupied with their own fabrications.

19 The manifestation of religion includes mystery, warning, enlightenment, and nourishment; these are symbolized by darkness, thunder, lightning, and rain. The ungrateful are mostly concerned with ignoring the warning, for fear that it will prove true against them. What they do not realize is that reality encompasses them and judges them whether or not they are consciously attentive of this fact.

20 The clarity of divine revelation is blinding to the eye accustomed to the darkness of human confusion. With each renewal of revelation, or revival of true knowledge, humanity makes some progress; when the infusion of inspiration subsides, however, humankind again stagnates. Although this process seems uncertain and erratic, at least humanity has a chance to use its God-given faculties to recognize revelation and live in its light; it is not the same as if we had no sense at all.

22 "So do not suppose anything to be like God, when you know": Knowing that God is the unique source of all creation, do not equate the Creator with any created thing.

30 "a deputy on earth": i.e. Adam/humankind. Note the angels' opinion of the human race.

31–33 According to the great sheikh Ibn al Arabi, the nature of the human constitution, represented by Adam, the first man, is distinguished by the integration of all existence, which is represented by God teaching Adam all the names or qualities comprising the universe. The angels, while having highly refined perception, do not have this integrated nature and thus lack complete knowledge.

34 The arrogance and ingratitude of Ibliis, the insolent angel, in refusing to follow the celestial design, is the model of the human fall into error through conceit. Ibliis thus became the personification of the Devil.

35 “you would become abusive tyrants”: They would do so by misusing knowledge and arrogating to themselves the will of God. “Abusive tyrants” renders the active participle of the first measure of the root DH-L-M, which means to wrong, to injure, to be unjust, oppressive, or tyrannical toward anyone, to misuse. From the same root is also derived *dhulma,* “darkness,” often used in a sinister sense.

36 Note that in the Quranic recollection Adam is not seduced into the fall by his wife, as in the familiar Judeo-Christian version of this story; in the Qur’an, Adam and his wife are both duped by the insidious suggestion of the devil (“the Obsessor”), the whispering of perversity and obsession.

“Let you all descend . . .”: Humankind would no longer live in the lofty innocence of the Garden.

“with enmity among you”: Being in a condition of alienation from each other as from our common source.

37 Here again the revelation in the Qur’an differs from Judeo-Christian tradition in its image of Adam. Earlier revelation focuses on the weakness of human nature and the need for atonement; the Quranic revelation focuses on the ever-present reality of atonement, the power and mercy of God, in restoring Adam to sanity and making him the first Messenger.

38 Like Adam and his wife, all humankind leaves the state of pristine innocence but is presented with the possibility of returning to the source by following intimations of truth emanating from it.

43 “Worship” here is a free rendering from R-K-!, which literally means bow down, a physical representation of surrender to the will of God.

44 The great Buddhist text known as *The Flower Ornament Scripture* expresses a similar idea: “Like someone on a corner saying all sorts of fine things while having no real inner virtue—such are those who do not practice” (Book X).

48 One of the most powerful images of judgment day is that of being utterly alone in the presence of Truth without any of the familiar supports of ordinary life.

62 See verse 256 of this same chapter: "There is to be no compulsion in religion." It is not certain exactly who these Sabians were; Penrice says they considered themselves followers of the prophet Noah. As Islam spread over the globe after the passing of the Prophet Muhammad, the term "Sabian" seems to have been understood, depending on the time and situation, to include other great Eastern religions like Zoroastrianism and Buddhism. The primary verb from the root S-B-' means to rise, as of a star. This may be the source of Penrice's idea that the Sabians worshiped the heavenly bodies. Using the sense of the root as referring to rising stars, the name and the image of revering celestial bodies might also figuratively represent followers of remote "lights" or revelations that were more distant from the early community of Islam than were Judaism and Christianity.

83 This verse, of which I have only translated a part, contains a beautiful summary of a believer's relationship to God and to humankind.

84–85 These verses have specific historical events as points of immediate reference, but they are addressed to all humanity and give a general description of a specific pattern in human history. This is a common device in the Qur'an. Only the first part of verse 85 is rendered here.

87 The invocation of the divine origins of the teachings and the perverse human psychology of recalcitrant peoples is repeated many times in the Qur'an. A key phrase here is "what your selves do not desire" (*maa laa tahwaa anfusukum*). People tend to reject what does not reinforce the sense of self or fulfill immediate desires.

The expression "haughty and arrogant" renders the verb from the tenth measure of K-B-R, having the senses of being haughty or proud, considering oneself (too) great (for something), and also of considering something important. The reference is to people making too much of their own selves and their own desires to be able to accept objective truth. The degree to which people have invested in their subjectivity shows in the vehemence of their reaction to Messengers and their messages: "Some you have branded liars, others you have killed."

90 "wrath upon wrath": This verse describes the ill fate of proprietary interest in religious dispensation: those who have received a revelation incur "wrath upon wrath" when they become possessive and jealous, because their attitude not only prevents them from receiving the benefit of the clarifications of new revelation, it also prevents them from fully appreciating the inner content of the earlier revelation, because of focus on human proprietors or proprietorship, and consequent forgetfulness of God, the source.

102–103 This passage gives one of the most sobering pictures of abuse of knowledge. I have omitted the opening of verse 102, which is a continuation of 101, speaking of misguided people following the gossip of obsessives about King Solomon's power. This gossip was evidently about magic, or the operation of knowledge beyond the boundaries of that necessary for mere survival in everyday life. The Qur'an defends Solomon and distinguishes him from obsessives and perverts, manipulators who "taught humanity magic," which operates through suggestion and obsession, and "what came down to the angels at Babylon," or extraordinary knowledge in the custody of powerful people of ancient times.

There is some question about the meaning of "angels" here; it comes from the root M-L-K, as does the word "king." Root meanings include having power or being able, and there are many derivatives concerned with mastery and dominion. Haaruut and Maaruut, and Babylon, seem to stand for extra–ordinary knowledge that "leaked" to the general run of humanity: at first it was made clear that this was a test, by which people could either prove the omnipotence of God beyond doubt or ruin themselves by abuse; then the "leak" got out of hand, and with the original caveat forgotten, people chose certain things for themselves, with disastrous consequences because of the incompleteness of their knowledge and the obsessive nature of their interests. They "had no share in the hereafter" because of this very tendency to indulge obsessively in manipulation of the things of this world. Thus humanity made magic a ruinous toy, forgetting the origin and total context of all knowledge.

"But then, however, they learned from the two what would separate man and wife": While there are forms of magic dealing specifically with creating and/or destroying human relationships, I am inclined to think that this passage may refer more generally to obsessive pursuit of knowledge and power, through which the man gets involved in trying to control and manipulate the world, becoming alienated from the nurturing matrix of earth and family represented in the woman.

"they hurt no one thereby except by leave of God": Free will is part of God-given human nature: without free will there would be no "trial" or "test," no means for humanity to awaken and become conscious of its God-given potential.

"those who bought it had no share in the hereafter": Those who acquired harmful knowledge, or became devotees of harmful magic, cut themselves off from reality by obsession with their fascinations and ambitions.

103 The powers that extraordinary knowledge offer humanity can diminish or enhance respect for the power of God, and can deflect or boost the ascent of the soul toward God. Because God is the source of all power, the rewards of exclusive worship of God outweigh those of devotion to any specific form of knowledge or power.

136 "for we submit to God": Islamic acceptance of the whole Abrahamic tradition is not based on mere historical heritage but on the recognition of the divine origin of the inspiration and prophecy from which it derives.

164 Many of the oaths in the Qur'an are sworn by natural phenomena. The laws of nature are viewed as signs of God, evidence of a living cosmic intelligent power.

177 Here is one of the most beautiful summaries of essential Islamic beliefs and practices.

"It is not righteous that you turn your faces east and west": This seems to mean that the heart of religion is not defined by superficial profession or allegiance as defined in terrestrial terms. Some translators render the *wa* here as "or," but the more usual "and" seems to me to be more inclusive and thus more suggestive of the transcendental aspect of devotion even as it is practiced within everyday life. The treasured Light Verse (included in this selection of readings from the Qur'an) says that the light of God is like a lamp alight with oil from a "blessed olive tree" that is "neither of the east nor of the west."

"for love of God" (*!alaa hubbihi*): This can also be read "in spite of love for it (goods/money)." The original uses a pronoun that can be construed either to refer to God or to wealth. Thus the passage can be read to speak of giving goods and money for love of God (as opposed to giving for personal motives), or of giving goods and money in spite of holding them dear (rather than just giving away what you don't care about). Together these meanings also express the Buddhist doctrine of the "emptiness of the three spheres" in perfect giving, which is said to transcend attachment to three spheres of feeling or conception: oneself as a benefactor, another as a beneficiary, and a gift as a benefaction.

255 This is the treasured Throne Verse (*'Aayat al Kursiy*), depicting God as the unique living reality minding the cosmos.

256 There *is* no compulsion in (real) religion because truth *is* objectively distinct from error by its own nature. The essence of error is idolatry, which means treating something relative as if it were absolute.

262–265 Here again are some exceptionally clear and concrete representations of what Buddhists call the "emptiness of the three spheres" in perfect charity. Real generosity is not calculating. Once a dervish, a Muslim religious mendicant, went to a barber in Mecca and asked for a shave. The barber, who was at that time working on a paying customer, immediately agreed and gave the dervish a shave. Impressed by this pious generosity, the dervish returned later with a purse of gold someone had given him as alms. The barber refused payment, saying, "Are you not ashamed to offer money for something done for the sake of God?"

285–286 According to tradition on the sayings and usages of the Prophet Muhammad, he said that if one recites these last two verses of "The Cow" in a night, they will suffice. (*"Al aayataani aakhiri suurati l baqarati man qara'a bihimaa fii laylatin kafataahu."*) (Bukhari, *Sahhiih*.) These beautiful prayers bear the fragrance of genuine humility before Truth.

285 This verse reaffirms the supreme focus on God, the Truth to which all genuine Messengers refer.

286 This verse reaffirms the precise justice and fairness of the Real, which tries and proves the individual soul through the interaction of its innate potential and the influences of the opportunities it has and the choices it makes.

The Family of Imraan ('Aal-i !Imraan) (Chapter 3)

This chapter was revealed at Medina. Imraan was the father of the prophet Moses; this chapter pursues the thread of the prophetic tradition and its essential teachings.

2 "the Self-subsistent" (*al Qayyuum*): or "The Eternal." This is one of the epithets of God and is an intensive derived from the root Q-W-M, with the essential meanings of to remain standing, to be, to exist. This epithet pairs perfectly with *al Hayy*, The Living.

3 "the Criterion" (*Al Furqaan*): This is a name of the Qur'an, especially in its function of distinguishing the original truth from false accretions in earlier revelations as they had come down through history. The name is derived from the root F-R-Q, which begins with basic meanings of to separate or divide, hence make a distinction, differentiate, discriminate.

7 Pursuing subjective interpretation of ambiguities is not rejected, it would seem, as pursuit of knowledge in itself, but insofar as interpretation involves projection of biases and attempts to undermine accord and cause division.

18 Absolute Truth Itself, the Real, bears witness to, or proves of itself, Its uniqueness.

19 This verse depicts those whose learning makes them conceited before people rather than humble before God, and those who come to value their own ideas and opinions more than truth itself.

"God indeed is quick to take account": The veiling of the rejecting mind is immediate in the act and posture of rejection itself; the consequences go on from there.

30 When the veil of falsehood is dropped, Truth is self-evident.

42 This selection introduces an elegant summary of the mission of Jesus. According to the Gospel of Mary, the mother of Jesus was a descendant of a priestly family whose lineage traced back to

Imraan, the father of Moses and Aaron. The only daughter of a priest with no sons, Mary was a temple virgin; she and especially Jesus are important figures in the Qur'an.

45 The Qur'an refers to Jesus as the Logos and the Messiah, and also a Spirit (or Breath) from God. The "Intimates" are those closest to God.

60 That is, divine revelation is not a human fabrication and cannot be treated adequately in the same manner as humanly fabricated ideas.

79–80 Elsewhere in the Qur'an, Jesus is asked by God whether he told people to worship him instead of God. The angels are similarly questioned, and so are all the prophets, as well as anyone to whom knowledge has come.

"It is not for a human being . . .": It is not the proper prerogative of a prophet (who remains a human being in spite of the high station of prophethood) to expect or demand to be worshiped.

"Rather be learned in divine law" (*kuunuu rabbaaniyiina*): Messengers or teachers of divine law, or knowledge of the divine, should themselves be followers of the divine, not claimants to divinity.

"one would not instruct you to take the angels or prophets as lords": A prophet faithful to the trust of God would not interpose other objects of worship, be it the person of a prophet or subtle beings. Buddhist teaching similarly says, "Rely on the truth, not on personality" (*Mahaparinirvana-sutra*). The Muslim theologian Al-Ghazali also wrote, "Judge people by truth, not truth by people" (*Kitaab al !Ilm*, "The Book of Knowledge").

105 "those who divide and differ after clarifications have come to them": This refers to the Qur'an in its function of clarifying earlier revelations.

137 The Qur'an repeatedly urges people to study the history of the world to observe the consequences of various attitudes toward life.

186 "You will surely be tested in your possessions and your selves": Our possessions and our selves are tests, or trials, to determine what use we will make of our endowments, which are ours on loan. The word for "test" is *balaa,* which means to try, prove,

experience. Our possessions and our selves are tests of how we manage them; we inevitably go through ups and downs in our material and psychological fortunes, and we never have everything entirely our own way. In all of these respects we are sure to be tested. There is also the specific message to the early Muslims that the new community was certain to be attacked, both physically and psychologically, by jealous conservatives of older dispensations, as well as by materialists who were threatened by the message of God regarding the nature and status of worldly things. This level of interpretation of the passage might also be taken as a general description of typical events accompanying any social reform.

"you will surely hear many insults": Addressed to the early Muslims, this also refers again generally to possessiveness and jealousy in religion, or automatic conservatism in matters of knowledge and culture.

"that is the resolve which will determine affairs" (*inna dhaalika min !azmi l'umuur*): Patience and conscientious reverence toward God constitute the resolve (*!azm*) that determines (*!azama*) affairs (*al'umuur*) because these spiritual strengths outlast and thus overcome material and physical trials.

190 "those of heart" (*'uuluu l'albaab*): The word *'albaab* is the plural of *lubb*, which means the heart, understanding, intellect, mind, reason. It is also interesting to note that *lubb* with the plural *lubuub* means core, pith, gist, essence, innermost.

195 "you come from one another": According to Jalaalayn, this means that men come from women, and vice versa; and that men and women are equal in respect to the right to compensation for work as well as the obligation to avoid squandering their earnings vainly.

Women (al Nisaa') (Chapter 4)

This chapter was revealed at Medina.

1 "by whom you ask of one another": Husbands and wives are to ask one another for sexual intercourse, in the name of God.

"be reverent toward relationships": The word for "relationships," *al arhaam*, specifically means blood relations; it also means wombs. Words for kindness, compassion, and mercy also come from the same R-H-M root. The general idea of the verse is respect for the sacred nature of human relations, including sexual relations and procreation.

3 According to Lady Aisha, wife of the Prophet and Mother of the Faithful, this passage forbids men to marry orphan girls with property just for their wealth, without providing a fair dowry. A "ward in your custody" originally meant a slave, a prisoner of war.

4 The dowry is for the woman's economic independence; a man is obliged to provide this even if his bride is already wealthy. If she is well-off and has no need of the dowry, she may voluntarily give some or all of it to her husband, but this decision is hers alone.

5 This provides for the care of those without substance or means, unable to care for themselves.

6 These are instructions for guardianship and disposition of the hereditary property of orphans: those not themselves in need should take no remuneration for guardianship, while poor people responsible for orphans are entitled to receive a fair recompense for looking after their affairs. In no case should guardians hastily consume the property of orphans in an attempt to enjoy it as much as possible before the orphans come of age and are eligible to receive their inheritance.

7 The portions for men and women differ because a family man is obliged to support others, while a woman is not.

8 There is also a provision for making acts of charity from a bequest according to the circumstances and needs of the situation.

9 Care for the affairs of orphans just as you would want your own children looked after should you yourself meet an untimely end and leave them orphaned.

28 As a mortal, transient being, the human is constitutionally weak. As a subjective consciousness susceptible to emotional upset, conditioning, and dependency, the human is psychologically weak. The ways of life described in sacred law are means of managing these weaknesses more easily.

29 "And do not kill yourselves": Here, "yourselves" means each other, emphasizing the unity of the believers, and also the unity of humanity as a whole, which God "made from one soul."

48 God does not pardon idolatry, or association of anything with God, because that association is itself diversion of attention that inherently alienates the individual from God. Hence verse 50 says, "That is sufficient in itself to be an obvious wrong."

53 Do idols and false deities have any role in the operation of the real universe? Idols and idolators give people nothing; they only take from people.

97 When people compromise themselves, they may seek excuses from their situation, without having explored their real alternatives.

125 The way of Abraham means acceptance of the absolute reality alone as God. The expression "seeking truth" is a paraphrase of *ḫaniifan*, "inclining," a name given to seekers of absolute truth in Muhammad's time.

164 Islamic tradition has it that there have been 128,000 prophets on earth, and 104 revealed Books. The Torah, the Psalms, the Gospel, and the Qur'an are considered the four most important of these Books from the point of view of Islamic tradition. Not all of the prophets were major public figures like Moses, Jesus, and Muhammad. The Qur'an says, "And We certainly sent Envoys before you (Muhammad); some of them We have told you about, and some of them We have not told you about" (50:78).

171 "do not go to excess in your religion": One of the Prophet's companions narrated that he never saw the Prophet so angry as on an occasion when he heard that a certain Imam was prolonging the morning prayer so much as to make it tiresome to others.

"a Spirit from God": In reference to Jesus as "a Spirit from God," the word spirit renders *ruuḫ*, which means breath of life or soul. Elsewhere the word "spirit" (or "sprite") renders *jinn*, "genii," and must be distinguished from this Spirit from God, which was Jesus. The Qur'an affirms the uncompromised unity of God without diminishing the dignity of Jesus the Messiah as a Word, Spirit, or Breath of Life from God.

The Table (al Maa'ida) (Chapter 5)

This chapter was revealed at Medina.

46 According to the Gospel, Jesus said the revelation he brought was not antagonistic to earlier revelation but in fact verified its truth. The Qur'an acknowledges this mission of Jesus and similarly presents itself as verifying and clarifying the essential message of the earlier revelations transmitted by Jews and Christians.

48 "and do not follow their desires": That is, do not follow the desires of the rebellious, who do not judge by what God has revealed.

Cattle (al 'An!aam) (Chapter 6)

This chapter was revealed at Mecca.

2 "then decided a term": The word "term" renders *'ajal,* which means a fixed term or predetermined period. Here it refers to a term for the evolution of the individual and a term for the evolution of the human race.

42–48 These passages provide a model of *fitna,* "trial," by both adversity and felicity, including the reflections by which humanity can make the best use of trial. Those who were "seized" with "misfortune and affliction" were "the communities before you."

50 These are instructions to Muhammad, and by extension to any prophet or religious teacher, to avoid interposing himself between God and humanity as an object of worship, and to refer all truth to its real source.

52 "seeking the essence of God": The word for "essence" here, *wajh,* also conveys meanings of being, countenance, aim, goal, objective, sense, meaning, favor, honor, sake.

53 The distinction between the spiritual elite and the social elite is also a test for the self-esteem of the social elite.

116 This verse highlights the distinction between subjective imagining and objective reality.

117 The great Sufi Najmuddin Kubraa used to say, "Truth alone knows what is true."

122 "for the ungrateful what they have done is made to seem pleasing to them": This describes the nature of habit, obsession, and self-delusion.

130 "spirits and humanity" (*al jinn w al 'ins*): The jinn, like humanity, differ among themselves in their quality of character and heedfulness of God.

"the meeting of this day of yours": This expression refers to the day of resurrection and judgment.

"Vain hopes": This refers to ingratitude to God because they confuse the imaginary with the real.

159 Those who fragment religion substitute the human for the divine; their opinions and allegiances assume greater importance to them than the unique reality of God.

160 "For those who do good is ten times that much": The reward of good is ten times what it merits; this is attributed to the pleasure and grace of God, the epitome of generosity and beneficence.

The Heights (al 'A!raaf) (Chapter 7)

This chapter was revealed at Mecca.

6 "We will question the messengers": They will be questioned as to whether they delivered their messages, and whether they claimed anything for themselves, such as divinity.

11–25 The story of the fall of humanity is retold here from a different angle, based on the fall of Ibliis, whose marks of prejudice, arrogance, and vindictiveness are illustrated. The devilish use of vain hope and self-consciousness to cause the downfall of the first humans is also made explicit here.

23 "We have oppressed ourselves": Humanity alienates itself from its source through the delusive action of its own obsessive self-absorption.

24 "Descend" from the state of innocence.

"enemies of one another," being self-conscious and therefore competitive and contentious.

25 "but you will be taken out of there": Life and death in the world are a temporary trial; the final return to ultimate truth takes the soul beyond the realm of worldly life and death.

36 "the inhabitants of the fire": The hell-bound, or the inhabitants of hell; that they "remain therein" is their own responsibility, as indicated by the present active participle in the original, because they create the conditions for hellish torment of their own free will.

87 "what I have been sent with": Here "I" refers to the Prophet; "what (he) has been sent with" refers to the message, the Qur'an.

157 "the Unlettered Prophet" (*an Nabiy al 'Ummiy*): Muhammad is known as the Unlettered Prophet. He neither read nor wrote. This literally and figuratively represents his innocence and purity of mind. It was by virtue of this innocence and purity that he was receptive to the message of God and was enabled to bear it to his people. The reference to Muhammad in the Torah is said to be in Deuteronomy 18; the Paraclete of Christian tradition (John 14) is also believed to be Muhammad the Prophet.

172 "AM I NOT YOUR LORD?": Remembrance of its origin and ultimate end lifts humankind from the idolatry of attachment to temporal things and human inventions.

177–181 God's creation provides faculties and facilities for both understanding and confusion, including the perception, reason, and free will by which humankind is enabled to choose between the "two highways" or the two possible uses of these facilities—the way of enlightenment and the way of delusion. Those who are like beasts are "even more astray" because the beasts do not have the choice afforded humans.

204 "the Recital" means the Qur'an.

206 "bow to God": This is a "verse of prostration," on the recitation of which the earnest reciter or reader bows to God.

Taa Haa (Chapter 20)

Revealed at Mecca. This is one of the earliest chapters of the Qur'an.

The Prophets (al 'Anbiyaa') (Chapter 21)

This chapter was revealed at Mecca.

2 Buddhist psychology speaks of a "barrier of knowledge" (*jnaanaavarana*) consisting of the impression that one's existing knowledge is complete and definitive.

3 "And they keep their conferences secret": Those who abused and oppressed the prophets and their followers were acting on private prejudice, not openness and impartiality. They try to make it appear as if the Message is coming from a human being, and one who is deranged or possessed at that. The fifth verse continues the litany of subjective ideas used as excuses invoked for ignoring divine communications.

7 The Qur'an repeatedly affirms that the prophets were human, to counter the belief or accusation that they claimed higher status than that. It also affirms that prophets are inspired by God, to counter the idolators' belief that the humanity of a Messenger disproves the divine source of the Message.

12 The trial of the world is not surmounted by trying to avoid it, but by living life as best we can, so that we may find out who we are in the process of taking responsibility for our lives and destinies.

16 "And not in play did We create": The processes of life and death and nature are not random or meaningless events: even if we regard them as meaningless, that act of choice does effectively have meaning, with implications for our future.

17 "Had we wished to take to sport . . .": Had God desired amusement, it would have been of a celestial rather than an earthly nature. The use of the relative lowliness and crudity of mundane existence as a proof of higher and more subtle meaning is one that is particularly arresting because of the apparent paradox.

18–19 "those in the presence divine are not too proud to worship God": Again the highest spiritual states accessible to humans, spirits, and angels are subordinated to the infinite reality of God, the Absolute; and their illumination shines with this very realization.

21 "Have they taken to gods . . .": The subject shifts; here "they" refers to humankind.

22 "beyond what they describe": Or, "beyond what they assert." The verb is the first measure of W-S̲-F, "to describe, assert." The point is the realization that God, or Reality, is beyond all human assertions and descriptions.

26 "Yet they say, 'The Compassionate One has gotten a son' ": This refers to the apotheosis of the prophet Jesus in sectarian Christianity.

26–29 "No, they are but honored servants": Jesus and the other prophets are not considered divinities, but "honored servants" of God.

34 "If then you will die, are they to be here forever?": The Prophet will die, like all prophets before him, but so will the persecutors of the prophets.

37 "Humankind is made of haste": Human beings are impatient by nature; this is part of the "trial," by which they may feel compelled to take on more responsibility than is possible for them.

44–45 "Do they not then see that We affect the earth?": Human kingdoms and empires wax and wane, none of them gaining permanent dominion. Peoples with the collective witness of long histories and traditions should be that much the more aware of the changeability and impermanence of earthly domains.

Light (al Nuur) (Chapter 24)

This chapter was revealed at Medina. I begin my selection from the famous Light Verse, one of the most prized of all passages from the Qur'an. The earlier verses of this chapter deal with social mores, including themes of chastity, privacy, modesty, and keeping innocent of vicious gossip.

36 "in houses which God has allowed to be raised": The word "raised" may be understood in the concrete sense of "set up," meaning houses of devotion built especially for constant remembrance of God; and the abstract sense of "elevate," meaning houses ennobled by constant remembrance of God.

37 "people who are not diverted": Some take this to refer to people who leave off worldly occupations to devote themselves completely to remembrance of God; others take it to refer to people whose worldly occupations do not distract them from constant and complete devotion to God.

39 "their works are like a mirage on a plain": Works emanating from human folly are based on subjective considerations and thus ultimately prove objectively insubstantial.

40 "or like the darknesses": This again refers to the works of ingrates who refuse to acknowledge the source of all being. The ocean is their consciousness, the darknesses are layers of ignorance, the waves are impulsive imaginings, the waves upon waves are rationalizations of their imaginings, the clouds are biases and blind spots.

"if one stretched forth a hand, one would hardly see it": The ignorance and blindness of the ungrateful not only hinders them from acknowledging the ultimate end, it veils them from the truth of what is near at hand.

"whoever God gives no light has no light at all": All true knowledge is from Truth: subjective human imagination has no connection with ultimate reality.

Rome (al Ruum) (Chapter 30)

This chapter was revealed at Mecca. Rome (*Ruum*) here means the Byzantine Roman Empire, which was at war with the Persian Empire in the time of Muhammad's mission. The chief cities of Syria were taken from Byzantine rule by the Persians in 611, and Jerusalem was conquered and pillaged in 614–615. This would seem to be the defeat of Rome to which this chapter refers. In the 620s, however, the tide shifted, as predicted in the Qur'an, until the Byzantines emerged victorious in 628.

9 "see how those before them ended up": Societies more powerful, more populous, more prosperous, and more educated have already passed away, so no one can be secure because of power, personnel, wealth, or education.

"They were more powerful than these": Here "these" refers to contemporary people.

21 “that you may feel at home”: The verb is of the first measure of the root S-K-N, meaning to be still, be tranquil, be peaceful, remain calm, be reassured, trust, have faith, feel at home, live, dwell.

22 Cultural and racial differences have occasioned contention among those who honor themselves more than God; for those who honor the signs of God, in contrast, diversity is richness and a source of richness, a means whereby communities may learn to become more than the sum of their parts.

26 “all are obedient to God”: Everyone, even the recalcitrant and rebellious, is subject to the laws of nature.

28 “have you slaves”: God is beyond the power of all subordinate agencies.

37 “God expands and restricts”: People need not become complacent or despondent when the tide of their fortune goes up or down; by referring all affairs to God, they can attain equanimity.

39 “Whatever you give from excess profit that it may grow even more”: The inglorious rise and collapse of financial “empires” based on manipulation of money rather than production and distribution of necessary and useful goods would seem to confirm the truth of the Quranic disapproval of economic practices functioning as breeder reactors for excess profit.

41 “to make them taste some of what they did”: The ill consequences of misdeeds are to be viewed as lessons and warnings, that people “may turn back” from error.

51 “and they saw it yellowing”: Yellowing means withering, wilting, destroying green crops: when an ill wind withers their mundane fortunes, people uncertain of God are inclined to despair and deny the bounty of God.

59 “Thus does God stamp the hearts”: The word for “stamp” is from the first measure of the root T-B-!, which means to stamp, imprint, leave an impression; in the passive voice it means to have a natural aptitude or disposition. Vehement reaction to truth is characteristic of those who do not exercise the faculty of perception and discernment (suggested by the Arabic verb “know” !-L-M used here).

60 The mission of the Prophet is to deliver a revealed message, not to accommodate doubters and critics; therefore Muhammad is instructed to focus on truth and not be diverted by those who waver. A false prophet is one who seeks a personal following, not truth, and is therefore taken up by the demands of the "consumers" to whom he is trying to cater.

Luqmaan (Chapter 31)

This chapter was revealed at Mecca. It is named after an ancient sage whose words of advice to his son constitute a major part of the chapter.

10 "every noble pair": This way of referring to sexually propagated creatures includes a beautiful reminder of the nobility of mating and reproduction as part of the celestial design for earth.

12 "And if anyone is ungrateful, well, God is free from all needs": God is not in need of praise and service from humanity; humanity is in need of praising and serving God.

13 "For idolatry is a tremendous error": Throughout the Qur'an, idolatry (*shirk* or association or equation of anything or anyone with God) is the cardinal sin, because it is the essential expression of heedlessness of the absolute nature of God.

14 "their mothers carry them, sapped and weakened": According to tradition, someone asked Muhammad the Prophet who is most deserving of one's kindness. The Prophet replied, "Your mother." The questioner asked, "Then who?" The Prophet replied, "Your mother." The questioner asked, "Then who?" The Prophet replied, "Your mother." The questioner asked, "Then who?" The Prophet replied, "Your father."

15 "in a courteous manner" (*ma!ruuf*): This is the past passive participle of *!arafa*, "know," and so literally means "known," but this also brings with it the meanings of universally accepted, generally recognized, conventional, fitting, that which is good or beneficial, equitableness, kindness, friendliness, beneficence, courtesy. Here is it used adverbially. People are not enjoined to obey their parents unconditionally, because Truth is the ultimate point of reference ("Your return is to Me"); but we are required

to be kind and fair to our parents even if there is disagreement in principle.

19 "Adopt a middle course in your walk": The verb Q-S̲-D means to be moderate, to steer a middle course; it also has the meanings of intend, proceed straightaway, aspire, aim, contemplate, consider, purpose: so the expression used by Luqmaan suggests not only moderation and balance but also purposeful direction; act deliberately and purposefully, without going to extremes.

21 The Obsessor, or the Perverse One, or the Obstinate One, is the Whisperer of suggestion who endears people to their habits ("what we found our fathers at") to such a degree that they ignore all else.

23 "the nature of hearts" (*dhaat as-s̲uduur*): Or, "what is in all hearts."

25 People may superficially acknowledge that the universe came from somewhere and reflects a noble design, without really registering the grace of God in the heart.

27 The Buddhist classic *Flower Ornament Scripture* says, "The Buddha revealed to me a teaching called universal eye, which is the sphere of all the enlightened, revealing the practice of enlightening beings, showing the differentiation of the planes of all universes, showing the spheres of all truths together, the light purifying all lands, dispersing all challengers, crushing all demons and devils, making all beings happy, ilumining the hidden recesses of all beings' minds, communicating to all beings in accord with their mentalities, illuminating the turning of the wheels of the senses of all beings. And I have taken up that teaching of the universal eye, keep it in mind, apply it, and contemplate it, taking it in this way: even if it were being written by a collection of pens the size of the polar mountains with as much ink as water in the oceans, it could never be finished; it would be impossible to finish even a part of a single line of a single formula of a single principle of a single doctrine of a single chapter of the teaching. It cannot be even partially exhausted, let alone fully exhausted or comprehended" (Book XXXIX).

28 "Your creation and resurrection": "Your" is plural, referring to all humanity, which is "created from a single soul."

33 "and do not let delusion delude you": The Deluder, Al Gharuur, is another personified description of the devil. It is derived from the root GH-R-R, from which come *gharra,* delude, mislead, deceive, beguile, blind, dazzle; *ghuruur,* deception, delusion, conceit, snobbery, vanity, trifles, banality, peril; and *ghirra,* heedlessness, inattentiveness.

Sheba (Chapter 34)

This chapter was revealed at Mecca. Sheba was an ancient city or people of The Yemen in South Arabia, a prosperous population that was destroyed or reduced by a great flood, supposedly occasioned by the breaking of the great dam of ancient Yemen.

3 "And there is nothing smaller than that, and nothing greater, but is in a clear Book": Everything, on macrocosmic and microcosmic scales of existence, is encompassed in revelation. The Buddhist *Flower Ornament Scripture* says, "There is nowhere the knowledge of the enlightened does not reach. Why? There is not a single sentient being who is not fully endowed with the knowledge of the enlightened; it is just that because of deluded notions, erroneous thinking, and attachments, they are unable to realize it. If they would get rid of deluded notions, then universal knowledge, spontaneous knowledge, and unobstructed knowledge would become manifest. It is as if there were a great scripture, equal in extent to a billion-world universe, in which are written all the things of the universe. . . . Though this scripture is equal in measure to a billion-world universe, yet it rests entirely in a single atom; and as this is so of one atom, it is also true of all atoms. Then suppose someone with clear and comprehensive knowledge, who has fully developed the celestial eye, sees these scriptures inside atoms, not benefiting sentient beings at all, and with this thought—'I should, by energetic power, break open those atoms and release those scriptures so that they can benefit all sentient beings'—then employs appropriate means to break open the atoms and release the great scriptures, to enable all sentient beings to benefit greatly. Similarly, the knowledge of the enlightened, infinite and unobstructed, universally able to benefit all, is fully inherent in the bodies of sentient beings; but the ignorant, because of clinging to deluded notions, do not know of

it, are not aware of it, and so do not benefit from it. Then the Buddha, with the unimpeded pure clear eye of knowledge, observes all sentient beings in the cosmos and says, 'How strange! How is it that these sentient beings have the knowledge of the enlightened, but in their folly and confusion do not know it or perceive it? I should teach them the way of sages and cause them to shed deluded notions and attachments, so that they can see in their own bodies the vast knowledge of the enlightened' " (Book XXXVII).

34 "And We never sent a warner to a community but its affluent members say, 'We reject what you were sent with' ": According to the Qur'an, God has sent warners (*nadhiir*) to every people. The affluent members of a community are those with the greatest stake in the status quo, and they therefore typically reject any new message with which warners are sent.

37 "and they'll be secure in the chambers on high": They will be stabilized in lofty states of proximity to Truth. The "compounded reward" for faithful good works includes the naturally good outcome of that goodness, plus the enhancement of the spiritual state made possible by faith in action.

39 According to the teaching of Buddhism, even the smallest gift, when given freely, without attachment, results in incalculable reward.

40 "But they did worship the spirits": Some people worship genii, or occult powers, or unusual mental states.

43 "What is this but a man who wishes to deter you from what your fathers worshiped?": Buddha told people not to hold to practices or beliefs just because they were traditional. Abraham and Muhammad also represent such breaks from tradition into truth, from inherited habit to direct perception.

45 "and how was My denial!": Those who rejected the envoys of Truth were, as a natural result, denied Truth. One sense of the "how" seems to be that the shattering reality of denial by God is inconceivable to those whose thought is directed to vanities in denial of God's warnings.

46 "your companion" refers to Muhammad the Prophet.

52 "how could they be receptive from a state so remote": As explained in the following verses, the "state so remote" is estrangement from truth, resulting from habitual heedlessness and denial.

Yaa Siin (Chapter 36)

Revealed at Mecca, Yaa Siin is called the Heart of the Qur'an. It is named after the mystic letters of the first line, which some say represent the words *Yaa Insaan!* meaning "O human being!" addressed to Muhammad in his capacity as a Messenger of God.

2 "By the Recital": The Qur'an itself is considered the miracle evidencing Muhammad's mission as an Envoy of God.

8 "yokes on their necks": These might symbolize worldly desires, which cause vision to be diverted from the real destination.

9 "a barrier before them and a barrier behind them": These seem to refer to the future and the past, anxiety and regret.

"covered them over": God lets humankind imagine whatever it will of the universe.

"so they do not see" because their views inhibit vision.

19 "does it depend on your being admonished?": The meaning seems to be "your real problem is not merely the annoyance you feel at being admonished: it is a problem that is in your own character, whether it is pointed out to you or not."

20 "from the remotest part of the city": Only someone detached from the arrogant pretensions of the "company of the city" could perceive the truth of the Messengers, who were operating outside the "company's" own system of punishments and rewards.

36 "who created mates, all of them . . .": Complementarity is seen in the vegetable world, the animal and human worlds, and in worlds invisible to the naked eye.

68 "whomever We grant long life, We reverse in nature": Whomever is granted long life is at the same time deprived of strength; the incapacity of old age is likened to a reversion to childhood and infancy.

69 "We did not teach him poetry": When Muhammad first was visited by revelation, he feared that he was either going mad or

becoming a poet. In particular, "We did not teach him poetry" means that the Qur'an is not a result of Muhammad's having been steeped in ancient literature, as many detractors past and present have claimed.

75 That is to say, false gods will be brought forth to Judgment as "witnesses" against "believers" in them, and also (in the case of humans, spirits, or angels who caused or allowed themselves to be worshiped) as coconspirators.

78 "and he makes similes for Us": Arrogant humanity conceives of God in human terms and continues to project human foibles and limitations on God. In recent times it has even become fashionable to assert that God is a human creation; this is the "God" who was declared "dead" some time ago by popular modern theologians.

Iron (Chapter 57)

This chapter was revealed at Medina.

3 "the manifest and the hidden" (*adh Dhaahir w al Baatin*): This can also be rendered "The Outermost and The Innermost."

7 "for those among you who believe and who spend": To "spend" in this context means to spend of what one has in charity or other good works; sometimes it is referred to as "spending in the way of God." This usage is quite common in the Qur'an, illustrating the importance of contributing to the balance and welfare of society.

8 "if you are faithful believers": To believe and have faith in God is, ipso facto, already to participate in a preordained state of grace.

8/10 "What is the matter with you . . .": Or, "Why do you not . . . ?" or "What hinders you from . . . ?"

11 I stress the meaning of "noble" for *kariim* here because generosity is already expressed in the foregoing, and the idea of nobility suggests that neither the material nor the spiritual gain is the result of greedy, self-seeking actions.

12 "and by their right hands": Light will stream from their righteousness and good deeds.

13 "Turn back behind you to seek light" (*'rji!uu waraa'akum fal tamisuu nuuran*): Or, "Turn back yourselves to seek light." Seek the light of God not in the projections of your subjective consciousness but in the awareness of God, which is the unique power subtending the universe and every living thing. In Buddhist terms, this line strongly suggests the practice known as "turning the attention around to look back" (Chinese *huiguang fanzhao*), in which one switches the focus of attention from present objects to the very source of awareness. Using this exercise as an interpretative framework, the "wall" set up between these people and the light is the ego and the subjectivity of consciousness: the "door therein, within it mercy" is the surrender of the ego and the relinquishment of subjective views and attachments to objects; the "torment" that is "outside, in front of it" is entanglement in thoughts and things that occur to the mundane consciousness.

17 "the ages grew so long to them": Over a long period of time, people lost interest in ancient revelations, which they no longer considered relevant.

21 The original literally says "The Great Grace," which means the epitome of grace, deriving from a higher order of reality.

27 "But the monasticism they invented for themselves was not prescribed by Us for them": The Qur'an does not enjoin monasticism, and Muhammad the Prophet also said there should be no monkery in Islam.

The Spirits (al Jinn) (Chapter 72)

This chapter was revealed at Mecca. Jinn is apparently the source of the English word "genius." The Arabic word *majnuun,* technically a past passive participle of a first measure verb derived from the J-N-N root, means possessed by spirits in the sense of insane.

6 "Folly" *(rahaq)*: This is from the root R-H-Q and it also means oppression. In the first measure the verb means to cause to suffer; in the fourth measure it means to impose difficulties or afflict with troubles.

23 "except reporting from God and God's messages": A Messenger is "estranged" from God in the sense of being in the midst of

mundane life on earth; but that "exile" is for a purpose, that of remembrance and prophecy.

"wherein they remain forever": Eternal damnation is eternal from the human perspective, not the divine perspective.

Those Sent Forth (al Mursalaat) (Chapter 77)

This chapter was revealed at Mecca. "Those Sent Forth" is interpreted to refer overtly to winds, symbolizing the Messengers of God.

1 "sent forth gently": The word for "gently," *!urfan,* has many other meanings and nuances: justly, beneficially, kindly, in a continual series. As a noun, *!urf* also means tradition. The basic root is !-R-F, with the primitive meaning of knowledge. The messengers come with justice, benefit, kindness, and knowledge. I choose the sense "gently" to contrast with the "tempestuous storming" of the next line, referring to the Message that is initially presented gently as glad tidings, then storms against ingrates and hypocrites.

The Highest (al 'A!laa) (Chapter 87)

This chapter was revealed at Mecca.

13 "where they neither die nor live": This is one of the most telling descriptions of the nature of the experience of the "fire" of "hell."

19 "the books of Abraham and Moses": Again the truly quintessential and thus perennial nature of the fundamental Message is recollected by citing the ancient Hanifite and Jewish traditions as reflective of the same Truth.

Daybreak (al Fajr) (Chapter 89)

This chapter was revealed at Mecca.

1 "By the daybreak": The dawning of realization.

2 "Ten Nights": There are various interpretations: one is that it refers to ten nights of the season of pilgrimage to the sacred shrine at Mecca; another that it refers to the first ten years of Muhammad's mission as a Prophet, during which he was subjected to enormous oppression and most of his people remained in ignorance.

3 "the Even and the Odd": When Muhammad the Prophet fled Meccan assassins with his trusted companion Abu Bakr, at one point the two of them sought refuge in a cave. Their pursuers, close upon them, came to the mouth of the cave and were about to enter, where they would find the refugee Prophet and his companion. When Abu Bakr expressed his fear to Muhammad, the Prophet said, "Do you think we are alone? There is a third with us," referring to God. They were saved when the would-be assassins noticed a spider's web over the mouth of the cave and concluded that the refugees could not have taken cover in there. The Even ("Two") refers to the Prophet and his companion; the Odd refers to God.

Also, the Even and the Odd can be interpreted to refer to humanity (or all creatures) and God, as humanity comes in pairs ("even"), and God is unique ("odd").

25 "no one can inflict the punishment of God": God's is the ultimate power, and the final chastisement of God is an experience of an order beyond anything that any human mind can conceive.

26 "and no one can tie the bonds of God": Similarly, the closeness of God and the intimacy between God and accepted souls are experiences beyond anything in the world of ordinary sense or feeling.

27 "O soul, in satisfied peace (*yaa ayyuhaa n nafsu l muṯma'innatu*): The soul in satisfied peace, *al nafs al muṯma'inna,* is the fourth of seven stages of development of consciousness according to a Sufi system. The adjectives in verse 28, "pleased and accepted" (or "pleased and pleasing"), *raaḏiya wa marḏiyya,* represent the fifth and sixth stages. The seventh stage in the Sufi system is that of purification and completion, here evidently represented by admission to the company of God's devoted and entrance into the Garden.

The City (al Balad) (Chapter 90)

This chapter was revealed at Mecca, which is the very city to which it refers, the home town of the Prophet Muhammad, who is addressed as a free inhabitant of the city. Symbolically, this may refer to Security (*Salaama*) as the birthright of every soul, attained by surrender to the will of God (*Islaam*), which is realization of the true nature of the soul.

4 "We have created humanity in difficulty": The word for "difficulty," *kabad* ("trouble, misery"), comes from the root K-B-D. The first measure of the root means afflict severely, wear down; the second measure means to inflict; the third measure means to bear, suffer, endure; the fifth measure means to undergo, be exposed, endure, have to take something on oneself, bear a cost, take up the center or step into the middle of a situation, or be in the zenith. All together these derivative associations paint a vivid picture of the plight of humanity.

18–19 The company on the Right Hand (of God) are the people of salvation; the company on the Left Hand are the people of damnation.

Night (al Layl) (Chapter 92)

Revealed at Mecca.

21 "who will surely be pleased": This may be construed, as here, to refer to God's pleasure in the acts just described. It may also be read as "and (they) will surely be satisfied," referring to the reward of those who act in such a manner.

The Forenoon (al Duhaa) (Chapter 93)

Revealed at Mecca.

The Expansion (al 'Inshiraah) (Chapter 94)

Revealed at Mecca.

7 "So when you are finished, be diligent still": Never allow yourself to become complacent and self-satisfied, even when you have accomplished a task successfully.

8 "and be attentive to your Lord": Always remember the source of all success. The latter phrase, *wa 'ilaa rabbika fa rghab,* may be read "and direct supplications to your Lord," or "and ask (only) of your Lord," suggesting that one should not rely on worldly success or worldly support, even be it for further success and support.

Recite! ('Iqra') (Chapter 96)

Revealed at Mecca. The first five verses of this chapter were the initial revelation to Muhammad. "Recite" also means Read or Proclaim. This chapter is also called *al !Alaq*, "The Clot."

4 "who taught by the pen": This evidently refers to the Word, the Book, preeminently the Qur'an, as the instrument of revelation. It also refers to that which "wrote" all the "signs" of God in the universe.

6–7 "Humankind does indeed go too far in regarding itself as self-sufficient": Comparatively recent ideas of the world and universe as mechanical systems that humanity can alter with impunity and ultimately master reflect the truth of this Quranic description of human egotism.

19 "bow down and draw closer to God": This is another verse of prostration, at which the reader bows to God.

The Night of Power (al Qadr) (Chapter 97)

Revealed at Mecca. It seems to me that in the Night of Power, as the time of celestial communications, the darkness and silence of the "night" symbolize the cessation of human conceptualization; the "power" is the divine knowledge revealed to the mind thus rendered receptive to subtler experience.

The root for the word "power" is Q-D-R, which has many significant derivatives. The verb in the first measure of this root means to possess strength, power, or ability, to be master. The verb in the second measure means to appoint, determine, decree, ordain, value, cherish, enable. The verb in the fourth measure means to enable. The verb in the fifth measure means to be appointed, ordained, destined, decreed. The verb in the tenth measure means to ask God for strength or power. There are also naturally many nominal derivatives.

The Shock (al Zilzaal) (Chapter 99)

Revealed at Medina. This brief chapter is a vision of the Last Day.

6 "On that day humankind will go forth divided to be shown their works": The word "divided" renders *'ashtaatan*, from *shatta*,

"scattered, separated, manifold, diverse." The sense is that people will be divided into the specific spiritual states that they cultivated by their works in the life of the world. The separation of humanity into the Company of the Right Hand and the Company of the Left Hand, or the Companions of the Garden and the Companions of the Fire, the virtuous and the evildoers, is an example of this "going forth divided."

The Charging Mares (al !Aadiiyaat) (Chapter 100)

Revealed at Mecca. The charging mares seem to symbolize courage and dedication to the cause of truth even in the face of massive opposition.

The Calamity (al Qaari!a) (Chapter 101)

Revealed at Mecca. This chapter presents another vision of the Last Day and Final Judgment.

Vying for More and More (al Takaathur) (Chapter 102)

Revealed at Mecca.

4 "indeed, on the contrary, you will know": Those who are engrossed in the things of the world do not prepare for the transition of death; they do not register the ultimate unreality of these things. When they are actually dying, however, unlike now they will really know that their worldly strivings diverted their attention from a matter even more pressing.

5–7 "if you knew with certain knowledge, you would surely see hellfire": Certain knowledge is not theory but experience. Those who know with certainty the real price of a life of "vying for more and more" see hellfire burning in it even now.

The Epoch (al !Asr) (Chapter 103)

Revealed at Mecca. The title *al !Asr* means Time, The Epoch, and also The Pressing Out, The Wringing Out, and also The Afternoon. All of these associations together create an apt title for this short chapter, which projects a powerful vision of the human situation.

The Slanderer (al Humaza) (Chapter 104)

Revealed at Mecca. Materialism is generally considered a form of *shirk* or idolatry in Islam. Materialists who accumulate their wealth by routinely attacking others are among the most base. This can be done in many professions.

The Elephants (al Fiil) (Chapter 105)

Revealed at Mecca. As in Confucian, Taoist, and Chan Buddhist traditions, the Qur'an uses many historical and mythological events for metaphors. In historical terms, "Those with the elephant(s)" refers to an expedition against Mecca led by the colonial Abyssinian governor of The Yemen in the late sixth century, around the time of Muhammad's birth. Abyssinia in East Africa and The Yemen in South Arabia were rich in those days, and this expedition was reportedly a massive force. The custodians of the shrine at Mecca did not put up a defense, judging the invaders too powerful; but something natural or supernatural evidently occurred to drive the aggressors back. This story was undoubtedly very fresh in Muhammad's time, and it must have been to the Meccan Arabians something like what the story of the Divine Wind that drove away invading Mongol hordes was to the Japanese in the thirteenth century.

Metaphorically, this story represents the fate of annihilation that awaits those whose idolatry is greed for material wealth and temporal power, which must in any case be impermanent.

The Quraish (Chapter 106)

Revealed at Mecca. The Quraish, to which Muhammad himself belonged, were the most powerful tribe among the Arabs of Northern Arabia. As is well known, the Quraish were the traditional custodians of the Kaaba, the sacred shrine at Mecca, which is referred to here as "this house." This verse is a simple yet eloquent admonition against idolatry and materialism in the sense that it reminds the people to be grateful to the source of blessings rather than presume upon the blessings themselves as an inherited right.

Needs (al Maa!uun) (Chapter 107)

Revealed at Mecca.

5 "those who pray without paying attention to their prayers": Those who outwardly pray (or practice other formal religious observances) but do not act in the spirit of religion. Caring for the disenfranchised and the destitute is enjoined upon the faithful time and again in the Qur'an.

Help (al Nasr) (Chapter 110)

Revealed at Medina. When this passage is read in the historical context of the struggle of early Islam for its very existence and its ultimate triumph, it is particularly remarkable as a model of the spirit of amnesty and freedom from rancor and vengefulness. The word for "help," *nasr*, also means victory, which in this context is naturally attributed to help from God.

Flame (al Lahab) (Chapter 111)

Revealed at Mecca. Historically this chapter refers to an uncle of Muhammad nicknamed Abu Lahab "The Inflamed," on account of his hot temper. He and his wife were among the most vehement opponents of early Islam. Metaphorically this refers to the ultimate end of the qualities of anger and aggression represented by Abu Lahab and his wife.

2 "His wealth does not enrich him and does not profit him": The anti-idolatrous–antimaterialistic principle of Islam expressed in the Qur'an is not rejection or denial of the things of the world but rather proper subordination of things of the world to God as the ultimate Reality (*al Haqq*). That means that the wealth of the world is not good or bad in itself, but its yields depend upon its use.

Pure Truth (al 'Ikhlaas) (Chapter 112)

Revealed at Mecca. This is one of the most famous revelations in the Qur'an, regarded as a classic statement of the absolute unity of God.

2 "the Ultimate" (*as Samad*): This epithet of God also might be rendered as The Eternal or The Everlasting. From the root S-M-D come words with the meanings to betake oneself and to stand up or hold out against: God is the ultimate goal to which we betake ourselves, and God as absolute truth stands up against and holds out, infinitely, against any falsehood the human or demonic mind can conceive. The word *samadaaniy* from this root also means everlasting or eternal.

The Dawn (al Falaq) (Chapter 113)

Revealed at Mecca.

2 "from the evil of what it created": That is, from what the "dawn" (the act of creation) created. Take refuge in God from the ill of created things.

Humankind (al Naas) (Chapter 114)

Revealed at Mecca.

4 "insidious suggestion" (*al waswaas al khannaas*): "The Whisperer Who Hides Away" is a personification of the devil; the last line shows that this is not understood as an individual being per se but as a kind of influence that can work through human beings or through genii or sprites (translated here as "demons" in view of their delusive capacity).

Select Bibliography

Abdullah Yusuf Ali. *The Holy Qur'an: Text, Translation, Commentary.* Washington, D.C.: The Islamic Center, 1978.

Burckhardt, T., and Culme-Seymour, A., tr. *The Wisdom of the Prophets* (from Ibn al-Arabi's Fuṣuuṣ al Ḫikaam). Gloucestershire: Beshara Publications, 1975.

Cleary, T., tr. *The Flower Ornament Scripture: A Translation of the Avatamsaka-sutra.* Boston: Shambhala, 1984–1987.

Dawood, N.J. *The Koran, with Parallel Arabic Text.* London: Penguin Books, 1990.

Jalaluddin al-Mahalli and Jalaluddin al-Suyuti. *Tafsiir al Jalaalayn.* Beirut: Dar al Marefah, 1971.

Muhammad Abul Quaseem. *The Recitation and Interpretation of the Qur'an: Al-Ghazali's Theory.* London: Kegan Paul International, 1984.

______. *The Jewels of the Qur'an: Al-Ghazali's Theory.* London: Kegan Paul International, 1983.

Muhammad Ali. *The Holy Qur'an.* Lahore: Ahmadiyyah Anjuman, 1951.

Muhammad Muhsin Khan, tr. *The Translation of the Meanings of* Sahih Al-Bukhari. *Arabic-English.* Beirut: Dar al Arabia, 1970.

Penrice, J. *A Dictionary and Glossary of the Kor-an.* London: Curzon Press, 1979.

Pickthall, M.M. *The Meaning of the Glorious Koran.* New York: New American Library, 1963.

Seyyed Hossein Nasr. *Ideals and Realities of Islam.* London: Allen & Unwin, 1988.

______, ed. *Islamic Spirituality: Foundations.* New York: Crossroad, 1991.

Stade, R., tr. *Ninety-Nine Names of God* (from Al-Ghazali's *Al Maqsaad Al'Asmaa'*). Ibadan: Daystar Press, 1970.